GREAT ESCAPES

Escapes from Man-Made Disasters

Stephen Currie

LUCENT BOOKS®

THOMSON

GALE

San Diego • Detroit • New York • San Francisco • Cleveland • New Haven, Conn. • Waterville, Maine • London • Munich

On cover: Firefighters rescue a victim of the World Trade Center collapse.

LIBRARY OF CONGRESS CATALOGING-IN-PUBLICATION DATA

Currie, Stephen, 1960-
    Escapes from man-made disasters / by Stephen Currie.
       p. cm. — (Great escapes)
    Summary: Describes escapes from five different man-made disasters.
       ISBN 1-59018-277-4
       1. Disasters—History—20th century—Juvenile literature. 2. Survival after airplane accidents, shipwrecks, etc.—Juvenile literature. I. Title. II. Series.
       D421.C89 2004
       363.34'97—dc22
 	
                                                                                           2004000386

Printed in the United States of America

Contents

Foreword

THE NOTION OF escape strikes a chord in most of us. We are intrigued by tales of narrow deliverance from adversity and delight in the stories of those who have successfully skirted disaster. When a few seemingly chosen people are liberated from a fate that befalls many others, we feel that to some degree the larger injustice has been rectified; that in their freedom, a small bit of justice prevailed.

Persecution and disaster, whether in nature or from what has frequently been called "man's inhumanity to man," have been all too common throughout history. Fires, floods, and earthquakes have killed millions; enslavement, inquisitions, and so-called ethnic cleansing millions more. Time and again, people have faced what seems to be certain death and looked for a way out. The stories of these escapes reveal the emotional and physical strength of our fellow human beings. They are at once dramatic, compelling, and inspirational.

Some of these escapes have been entirely the work of one brave person. Others have involved hundreds or even thousands of people. Escapees themselves vary; some seek to return to a life they have lost, others flee to a life they have only dreamed of, still others are simply fugitives against time. Their stories enlighten even the darkest events of history, making it clear that wherever there is determination, courage, and creativity, there is hope. Dr. Viktor E. Frankl, a survivor of four Nazi concentration camps, expressed this tenacity in the following way: "Everything can be taken from a man but one thing: the last of human freedoms—to choose one's attitude in any given set of circumstances—to choose one's own way."

People who are mired in captivity become willing to chance the unknown at any cost. Americans who escaped from slavery, for example, escaped toward a vision that the life they had never been allowed to live would offer them new hope. Fugitive slaves had no inkling of what life in free territory would hold for them, or if they would even make it there alive. Fears of the unknown, however, were outweighed by the mere possibility of living a free life.

While many escapes involve careful and intricate planning, no path of flight follows a fixed blueprint. Most escapes owe their success to on-the-spot improvisation and keen resourcefulness. A piece of clothing found at a critical juncture might be just the thing out of which to fashion a cunning disguise; a brick lying harmlessly in the corner of a room might provide just enough support to boost a person through the crack in a window.

Conversely, fate may carelessly toss many pitfalls at the feet of those in flight. An unexpected flood might render a road impassable; a sympathetic train conductor might be suddenly fired, replaced with an unfriendly stranger. All escapes are both hindered and helped by such blind chance. Those fleeing for their lives must be nimble enough to dodge obstacles and snatch at opportunities that might affect their chances along the way.

It is common for people who have undergone such ordeals to question whether their salvation came to them by chance, or if they were somehow chosen for a greater scheme, a larger purpose. All become changed people, bestowed with a grand sense of purpose and a rich appreciation for life. It is this appreciation for life too that draws us to their stories, as they impress upon us the importance of living every day to its fullest, and inspire us to find ways to escape from our own prisons.

Lucent's Great Escapes series describes some of the most remarkable escapes in history. Each volume chronicles five individual stories on a common topic. The narratives focus on planning, executing, and surviving the escapes. The books quote liberally from primary sources, while ample background information lends historical context. An appendix of primary sources is also included in each volume, sharing additional stories of escape not profiled in the main text. Endnotes, two bibliographies, maps of escape routes, and sidebars enhance each volume.

Introduction

Man-Made Disasters

YEAR AFTER YEAR, some of the most dramatic stories reported in the media are those that deal with terrible disasters. Television viewers and newspaper readers alike seem drawn to real-life tales of people battered by forces beyond their control. In many ways, these stories are natural source material for front pages and news broadcasts. For the most part, they arise suddenly and often without any warning; their impact on a region or on certain people may last for several days, perhaps longer; and the struggle of those affected to protect their lives and property generally makes for compelling drama.

Some of the most dramatic among these stories describe disasters caused by natural phenomena, such as tornadoes, earthquakes, and volcanoes. These disasters serve as reminders that humans are not in control of their own world. Even the strongest buildings cannot reliably withstand 160-mph winds; high levels of rainfall can lead inevitably to floods, regardless of human attempts to dictate otherwise.

But perhaps the most compelling of disaster stories are those that describe catastrophes created by human intervention. These man-made disasters are the result of technology gone wrong. An airplane crash is one example of a man-made disaster. So are gas explosions at coal mines, electrical fires in factories, and the sudden collapse of bleachers at a sports event. The disaster may be caused deliberately, as in a terrorist attack or a fire set by an arsonist; or it may be accidental, such as an industrial accident stemming from unsafe handling of dangerous chemicals. But the effect is the same: because of human fallibility, disaster strikes.

A Dark Fascination

Man-made disasters, therefore, serve to remind people of their own limitations. The handiwork of humans, however ingenious or inspired, is not immune to destruction. Hastily constructed shacks fall down, but so too do billion-dollar skyscrapers. No jet is immune from crashing, no fortress is able to repel all attacks. Indeed, what attracts the most public attention is the failure of the biggest and strongest human structures. There is a dark fascination in reading about the sinking of a supposedly unsinkable ship, or watching a deadly fire sweep through a building billed as practically fireproof.

This fascination with man-made disasters is not confined to modern times. Throughout history, people have paid close attention to catastrophes of this sort. Disasters such as the Chicago Fire of 1871 and the sudden explosion of the American battleship *Maine* during the Spanish-American War made newspaper headlines from coast to coast. Although the *Maine* is no longer widely remembered, the Chicago Fire is one of many early disasters to remain famous today.

Some of the best-known disasters, in fact, belong today to popular culture, legend, or politics. The Triangle Shirtwaist Fire, an early twentieth-century blaze in which many New York factory workers died, quickly came to symbolize the

Then and Now

To a degree, man-made disasters are a function of modern times. The more humans act to create and shape the world around them, the more vulnerable they become when tragedy strikes. Skyscrapers are marvelous feats of engineering—but when they collapse, whether from terrorist attacks or from structural weakness, they put thousands of lives at risk. Today's commuter trains and jet airliners carry far more passengers than did wagons and horses of earlier centuries; thus, a single modern train wreck or plane crash can have a much greater impact than did accidents five centuries ago.

But in other ways, the effects of man-made disasters today are less significant than might be expected. As the danger has grown, so too has technological knowhow. For the most part, cars, trucks, and ships are safer than ever before, with more plentiful and more sophisticated safety devices. Twenty-first-century firefighters benefit from equipment unknown to their counterparts of a hundred years ago. And communication systems help alert people to the presence of danger, as well as speeding up the process of summoning assistance to the scene. Paradoxically, disasters of today are both more dangerous—and less deadly—than those of earlier generations.

inhumanity with which laborers of the time were treated. Disasters have been immortalized in music, art, and poetry; Gordon Lightfoot's song "The Wreck of the Edmund Fitzgerald" tells of a deadly Lake Superior shipwreck, while the folk song "Casey Jones," still sung today, commemorates a century-old train crash. And many people can recall exactly where they were on the day in January 1986 when the space shuttle *Challenger* exploded, killing all seven astronauts on board. In such ways, man-made disasters help create common bonds among people of disparate groups.

The space shuttle Challenger *explodes just after takeoff. The 1986 tragedy is just one of many man-made disasters that has captured the world's attention.*

Escapes

Some man-made disasters are exceptionally lethal. The *Challenger* disaster left no survivors. The crash of a passenger jet also may result in the death of all aboard. Other disasters, in contrast, may cause major environmental harm without directly killing any people. The 1989 wreck of the oil tanker *Exxon Valdez* in Alaska's Prince William Sound, for instance, fouled miles of coastline with oil and killed fish, birds, and marine mammals, but did not result in any human deaths.

Most man-made disasters, though, lie somewhere between these two extremes. While some victims of the catastrophe may be killed outright, others manage to escape death. The number of those who fall into each group depends in part on the type of disaster—a car crash, for instance, is typically less deadly than a mining accident. But even within categories of disasters, death tolls are not consistent. Some fires are more intense or spread more rapidly than others. Some ships are farther from shore when they sink. Weather conditions, geography, and the time of day can all play a role in determining the number of people who escape.

A handful of other factors are also important in determining who escapes from a man-made disaster. Among these are courage, resourcefulness, and the ability to think and act quickly.

Those who fail to seize the first chance they are given may forever lose the opportunity. In contrast, those who come up with backup plans and alternative ways out are more likely to survive. Many people who have escaped from man-made disasters have done so by bravely and forcefully fighting their way to safety.

But perhaps the most determining factor of all is chance. Most survivors of terrible disasters recognize that they were not in control of their escapes. They happened to be sitting in the part of the bus farthest from the impact, or they left the furnace room of the factory minutes before the boiler exploded. Some, however, attribute their survival to a greater power. "This is not about luck," says one woman who survived the terrorist attack on the World Trade Center. "This is about God having a plan."[1]

The five escapes described in this book include many examples of people who were lucky. They also include the stories of people who made decisions that clearly improved their chances of survival. The truth is that each is important. Whether evacuating a burning building, running from a toxic cloud, or abandoning a steadily sinking ship, a person needs plenty of good fortune—and plenty of good planning as well. Those who survived these five disasters, and others like them, generally had both.

1

Escape from the *Titanic*

PERHAPS THE MOST famous man-made disaster in history is the sinking of the ship *Titanic*, which went down in 1912 in the North Atlantic Ocean after a collision with an iceberg. Nearly a century after the accident, the story of the doomed ship remains well known. The sinking has been the subject of several popular songs, a Broadway musical, and a number of movies, among them one of the most successful films of the 1990s. The tragedy has spawned, in addition, museums, newsletters, clubs, and a steadily increasing library of books.

The story of the *Titanic* is best known for its tragic elements. Even today, most people are aware that the ship was widely considered unsinkable. Many know that the *Titanic* carried too

few lifeboats, that some third-class passengers had difficulty reaching the upper decks after the collision, and that hundreds of people died that night as the doomed ship gradually settled lower in the water. These parts of the story are certainly compelling, as are other aspects of the *Titanic*'s sinking that reflect the tragedy of the situation.

But there is another dimension to the tale of the *Titanic*. That is the fact that hundreds of people managed to escape death that evening—and did so under trying and sometimes terrible circumstances. Even though barriers like gates and locked doors at times made progress difficult, for example, the survivors nevertheless reached the main deck. Despite massive confusion that evening, they were able to board the lifeboats. And they managed to stay afloat throughout the bitterly cold night until rescue ships arrived the next morning. The escapes of these passengers were often remarkable; certainly, they were never routine. They are an essential part of the story of the *Titanic*.

The Largest Ship in the World

The *Titanic* was the brainchild of two wealthy British men, Bruce Ismay and James Pirrie. The two were acquainted through a mutual interest in business

and ships. Pirrie was a principal owner of a shipbuilding company known as Harland and Wolff, and Ismay was the managing director of the White Star Line—a British shipping firm with a particular emphasis on transoceanic passenger travel.

During the 1890s and into the first years of the twentieth century, both businesses had done well. The White Star Line was generally considered to have some of the best passenger ships in the world; most of them, in turn, had been constructed by Harland and Wolff.

The Titanic *plunges into the North Atlantic in 1912. The sinking of the massive passenger liner remains the most famous man-made disaster in history.*

But by 1907, Ismay and Pirrie had both begun to worry about the future of their companies. The White Star Line was no longer as dominant as it once had been. Other companies, both in England and Germany, had begun to put faster and more luxurious ships into service. Indeed, a competing English company had just launched a new passenger ship, the *Lusitania*, that outshone anything Ismay's firm had to offer.

Over dinner one evening in the summer of 1907, Pirrie and Ismay agreed to collaborate on a new project designed to win back their companies' earlier dominance. Their plan was simple, striking, and bold. Harland and Wolff would build two new passenger liners, both of them considerably larger and more comfortable than anything ever built before. Once they were complete, the White Star Line would run the new ships on regular routes between Britain and North America. If all went well, the ships would help the White Star Line reclaim much of its former market share, and Harland and Wolff would benefit from future contracts with Ismay's company.

The men's plans were big. But the ships they sketched out at dinner that evening were bigger still. Although the new ships would differ slightly in their dimensions, both would be considerably larger than the *Lusitania*. Where the *Lusitania* measured almost eight hundred feet in length, for instance, the new ships would be closer to nine hundred. The difference in weight was even greater: the new ships would weigh nearly forty-five thousand tons, compared to the *Lusitania*'s thirty thousand.

The names of the new ships, too, would indicate the vessels' size and majesty. The smaller of the two would be known as the *Olympic*, a name reminiscent of the powerful gods and goddesses of ancient Greece. And the larger of the two, designed to be the biggest ship of its time, was to be called the *Titanic*—a word that simply means "enormous."

"Unrivaled Extent and Magnificence"

Ismay and Pirrie quickly set to work planning and designing their new ships. The process was slow and drawn out; the *Titanic* would not be launched until 1911, and would not travel far from the shipyard until early 1912. But the delays only increased the excitement among potential passengers and the general public. The two massive liners, and particularly the *Titanic*, represented something novel—a sort of a supership, impressive beyond imagination. As construction neared completion, those who visited the *Titanic* in person found the sight breathtaking. "It towered high over the buildings," wrote a journalist, "and dwarfed the very mountains beside the water."[2]

Although the *Titanic* was fast, it was not built specifically for speed; the *Lusitania* could have defeated it in a race. What it offered instead was luxury, comfort, and grandeur. The *Titanic* had ballrooms, fine dining, chandeliers—even a squash court and a small

The Olympic *and the* Titanic, *shown here under construction in the Harland and Wolff shipyard in Belfast, were designed to dwarf other ships of their day.*

swimming pool. Elevators were available to whisk passengers from one deck to the next. Or they could use the grand staircase, capped by a dome made of wrought iron and glass.

The *Titanic*'s passenger accommodations were impressive too. Some luxury suites came with their own private walkways. A shipbuilding trade magazine raved that the staterooms were "of unrivaled extent and magnificence."[3] Like other ships of its time, most of these amenities were reserved for the first-class passengers. Even so, the second- and third-class quarters were considerably more comfortable than those of other transatlantic ships.

Luxury was a main selling point for the *Titanic*, but the ship promised another incentive to potential passengers as well: unparalleled safety. Those who worried about the possibility of a shipwreck during the long trek across the Atlantic seemed to have nothing to fear aboard the *Titanic*. Separate watertight compartments lined the sides of the ship, promising to keep it afloat even if water leaked into one or two of them. It was hard to believe that disaster could ever strike such an imposing vessel. White Star officials encouraged this perspective. "We believe

First- and Third-Class Passengers

Like virtually all methods of passenger transport at the time, tickets to board the *Titanic* were available in different classes. First class, the most expensive, was also the most luxurious; the nicest areas of the ship were reserved for the use of these passengers alone. Second-class tickets were cheaper, and the accommodations correspondingly less fancy. Third-class passengers traveled most cheaply of all, and were largely confined to quarters on the lower decks of the ship. The various classes' experiences aboard the ship were not the same, and neither were their survival rates. Well over half the first-class passengers were saved; less than a quarter of those traveling third class survived.

Part of the reason for the differences involved the layout of the ship. The third-class passengers had to escape by going up a maze of stairwells—a physically demanding trip under the best of circumstances, and particularly difficult once the ship began to sink. Part, also, had to do with individual decisions and choices. Later testimony suggested that third-class passengers were less likely to put on lifejackets than those in first class, and that many women in that part of the ship refused to go without their husbands.

But there are also indications that the odds were stacked against the third-class passengers. Several events and comments that evening suggested that crew members were making an effort, consciously or not, to increase the chances of first-class passengers' survival at the expense of the poorer travelers. At least one set of gates on the way upstairs from the third-class quarters, for instance, had unaccountably been locked—and despite the danger, the gates never opened.

Moreover, while some of the stewards in charge led third-class passengers upstairs, other crew members blocked some of the accessible stairways to make sure that the men below did not storm the decks. And one first-class passenger later claimed that a crew member had turned several second- and third-class passengers away from a lifeboat, explaining that the boat was for first-class passengers only. Though most historians do not believe there was a formal conspiracy against the third-class passengers, there is no doubt that shabby and inequitable treatment lowered the escape rate for the poorest travelers aboard the *Titanic*.

that the boat is unsinkable,"[4] the company's vice president once stated flatly.

Bound for New York

The combination of luxury, safety, and speed made the *Titanic* "the last word in modern efficiency,"[5] as one visitor to the ship put it. The combination also created great interest in the ship's maiden voyage. Newspapers and magazines ran extensive articles about the new luxury liner; people throughout England and much of the United States talked about its size and its prowess.

Given the hype, ticket sales were somewhat disappointing. When the ship left Southampton, England, on April 10, 1912, it was not nearly full. Even after two scheduled stops, one in France and the other in Ireland, the ship was only about two-thirds full. Still, a huge crowd had assembled in Southampton to watch the ship steam away from the harbor. Even with fewer passengers than anticipated, about thirteen hundred paying customers were on the ship when it began its crossing to New York.

The passenger total was increased considerably by the nine hundred or so crew members carried aboard the *Titanic*. This list included stokers, who shoveled coal into the mighty furnaces that powered the ship; stewards and stewardesses to serve the first- and second-class passengers; cooks, barbers, navigators, radio operators, and many more. In all, the *Titanic* had 2,201 people on board as it headed across the Atlantic Ocean to New York.

The first few days of the *Titanic*'s voyage went smoothly. The ship's path to New York largely followed standard shipping lanes across the North Atlantic. The route, however, could be dangerous, especially around the month

The Titanic *sets off on its maiden voyage with the help of a tugboat. The ship charted a dangerous course through the waters of the North Atlantic, where icebergs were fairly common.*

of April. Icebergs tended to float south from the Arctic during the early spring; they often could be seen in the ocean off Newfoundland in eastern Canada.

Although icebergs could look quite beautiful and even harmless in the bright light of day, experienced sea captains knew to steer clear of them. Ice was hard, unyielding, and jagged. Worse yet, most of the bulk of each berg was concealed under the surface of the water. Over the years, ice had destroyed dozens of ships, including some very large ones.

Captain Edward Smith of the *Titanic* did not believe that ice posed a serious threat to his ship. Like White Star officials in general, Smith viewed the *Titanic* as essentially unsinkable. Still, he was not inclined to take unnecessary chances. Learning from other captains by radio that the ice was unusually heavy in this part of the ocean, Smith steered a new course that would take the *Titanic* about ten miles south of the usual shipping lanes.

But that was the only precaution he took. On the night of April 14, as the *Titanic* approached the area of greatest reported ice, Smith did not order the ship to slow down and pick its way carefully through the scattered icebergs. And when night fell and visibility worsened, Smith assigned only two crewmen to watch for icebergs. Indeed, there is reason to wonder why Smith did not dip even farther south. According to information he received from nearby captains, his new position left him squarely in the middle of the ice field. Smith's

failure to take the ice more seriously would lead to tragedy.

The Crash

The night of the fourteenth of April was bitterly cold. By late evening, the near-freezing temperatures had driven many of the passengers into their bunks. A handful of people, however, continued to stroll on the decks. "It was all so quiet," remembered Violet Jessop, a stewardess aboard the ship, "but how penetratingly cold it had become!"[6] Still, those who remained outside also noted the beautiful clarity of the skies. "You could almost see the stars set,"[7] reported one crewman.

Despite the clear skies, though, the task of looking out for icebergs was exceptionally difficult that night. The two lookouts stationed in the crow's nest near the top of the ship had little to rely on in their search. Moonlight is helpful in seeing icebergs, but there was no moon that night. Moreover, the seas were unnaturally calm. Icebergs can sometimes be identified by waves breaking around their base, but the unusually still waters that night eliminated waves altogether.

At about 11:45 P.M., lookout Frederick Fleet suddenly spotted an iceberg dead ahead. He seized a telephone and informed the crew on the deck below. Quickly, those in charge of steering the ship swung the wheel around. Their hope was to turn the massive ship before it could strike the iceberg. And for a moment, it seemed to Fleet as if they would be successful. But then he heard a telltale scraping noise: the *Titanic* had hit the edge of the iceberg.

To most of the passengers on board the ship, the impact was hardly noticeable. "There was only a slight shock and bumping," reported passenger Jack Thayer. "Then all was still."[8] A few described the impact as a crash; Violet Jessop would later say that she heard a rip or a crunch from her position on the deck. But even Jessop did not immediately know what had happened.

The captain and the ship's officers knew, however, and word that the ship had collided with an iceberg spread quickly throughout the *Titanic*. Wakened by stewards and fellow passengers, people stumbled out of their beds to see what was going on. A few immediately assumed the worst. They hurried to get dressed, to gather their belongings, or to put on lifejackets. But most, noting that the impact had been mild and that the ship had quickly steamed on, thought that there was no danger. "This ship could smash a hundred icebergs and not feel it,"[9] exclaimed one woman.

The mood soon began to change, however. A third-class passenger awoke to find frigid water swirling around his feet. Several first-class passengers noted that the ship appeared to be gradually tilting as they strolled around the deck. As the *Titanic* slowed, more and more passengers began to lose their confidence in the ship's ability to withstand damage.

They had reason to be concerned. The jagged undersea edge of the iceberg had in fact raked across the ship's hull, cutting a long gash in the side. Water had immediately begun pouring into the lower decks of the ship—and into several of the watertight compartments as well. Despite their best efforts, crewmen were unable to stop the flow. Gradually, the ship's officers realized the truth: the ship was doomed.

To the Lifeboats

There was only one thing to do, and that was to evacuate the ship. Smith told his officers to alert the passengers and start putting them aboard the *Titanic*'s lifeboats. At the same time, he instructed his radio operators to send a distress signal. He hoped that a nearby ship would hear the call and come to pick up the passengers and crew.

Smith knew that the distress call was absolutely essential for survival. Aside from the freezing temperatures, which would make being afloat on the water extremely uncomfortable, there were two significant problems with relying on the lifeboats. The first was a lack of planning on the part of the crew. There had been no lifeboat drills, nor had anyone bothered to assign passengers to individual boats. The result, Smith knew, would be chaos on board the ship.

But the second problem was far more serious. The *Titanic* had just sixteen lifeboats and four smaller vessels known as collapsibles. Taken together, there was space for just 1,178 passengers and crew members. Even if every

Women and children are loaded into one of the Titanic's *lifeboats. The ship did not carry enough lifeboats for the two thousand passengers on board.*

boat left the ship smoothly and easily, over one thousand people would have no boat to board. Smith could only hope that the distress call was heard—and, in the meantime, that the ship would sink slowly.

Members of the crew now circulated among the passengers, banging on doors and shouting instructions. They ordered passengers to put on their life vests and hurry to the boats. Officially, they counseled patience and calm. "There are plenty of boats in the vicinity," Violet Jessop remembered an officer assuring the passengers. "They'll be with us any moment now."[10] But the orders seemed to contradict the soothing words. Quickly, passengers began to assemble on the deck.

What happened next was mass confusion. A few people immediately boarded the closest lifeboats, assisted by members of the crew who stationed themselves nearby. But most wandered around aimlessly, wondering what they should do. Still others had been separated from friends or relatives and were trying to find them in the assembled crowd. Many thought it would be unwise to climb into the lifeboats. "We are certainly safer here than in that little boat!"[11] remarked passenger J.R. McGough.

Boarding the Lifeboats

Still, little by little, passengers, mostly women and children, began to crowd into the boats. Indeed, in accordance with an old nautical custom, many of the officers responsible for the lifeboats refused to permit men to board until all the women were safe. To be sure, a few men did board the boats, some by special permission—generally these were new husbands, elderly men, and young fathers—and some because they were pressed into service to help row the lifeboats.

About an hour after the ship struck the iceberg, several of the boats were declared ready to go. All had been loaded haphazardly, and none were completely full. Most crew members erroneously believed that fully loaded boats would break. Moreover, they were not willing to wait while people decided whether to get in. Knowing the

The Lifeboat Shortage

The shortage of lifeboats aboard the *Titanic* was hardly unique to that particular ship. Very few ocean liners of the time provided anywhere near enough lifeboats to accommodate all passengers and members of the crew. Existing laws in England did force steamship companies to carry a certain number of lifeboats of a specified size, but the regulations did not require that the lifeboat capacity match that of the ship. The *Titanic*, in fact, did better than many other ships of the time. Its lifeboats provided space for 216 more people than the law actually demanded for a ship of its size.

The men who ran the great steamship lines said that providing lifeboats for everyone was unnecessary. Their reasoning had to do with the growing size of ocean liners and the advent of radio equipment. Any ship that managed to get into trouble would sink very slowly, they reasoned, which would give the crew time to radio an alarm to other ships in the area. In this scenario, the only role for lifeboats would be to ferry passengers off the sinking ship to the ones hurrying in

to make the rescue. There would be plenty of time to make two or three trips. Thus, there was no need to have lifeboat space for every single passenger and member of the crew.

The men who made this argument may well have believed it. But a more likely reason for the lack of lifeboats was financial. Space was severely limited aboard ships, even on one as large as the *Titanic*. Every square inch of the deck occupied by a boat meant one less inch for passenger cabins, lounges, or other amenities designed to increase comfort or capacity. The fewer lifeboats, then, the more tickets a steamship company could sell—and the more it could charge for each.

The *Titanic* should certainly have had a full complement of lifeboats. But the fact that it did not mainly reflected the prevailing sentiment of the time. After the tragedy, new laws were passed—in Britain and elsewhere—mandating full lifeboat coverage on large ships. It was too late for those who had gone down with the *Titanic*, but the laws would save countless others in later shipwrecks.

Once the lifeboats hit the water, the men who manned the oars rowed feverishly to move away from the sinking ship.

danger better than the passengers did, they believed that making haste was more important than cajoling reluctant passengers to climb in.

Once loaded, the boats were swung over the side of the *Titanic* and lowered gradually into the water. Despite their fears, some passengers found the descent from the ship fascinating. "It was thrilling to see [the] black hull of the ship on one side and the sea, seventy feet below, on the other," remembered one passenger. "Or to pass down by cabins and saloons, brilliantly lighted." [12] But most aboard the lifeboats were too busy being afraid to notice the beauty as they dropped to the ocean.

Indeed, few of the lifeboats managed to get away smoothly. One swung toward a spray of exhaust water from the ship; the stream would have tumbled all the passengers into the ocean. Fortunately, the people on the boat pushed themselves away from the exhaust before disaster struck. The ropes of some lifeboats tangled as they went down. Others were lowered too quickly or not quickly enough. Violet Jessop remembered her boat hitting the surface of the ocean with such violence that the craft was nearly turned over.

Once down, the crewmen released the boats from the ropes connecting them to the *Titanic*. Then the men—and occasional women—at the oars rowed quickly away from the ship while other passengers huddled together for warmth. Most of the people in the lifeboats kept a wary eye on the ship,

its lights still shining crookedly in the distance. Some cried, especially those who had left family or friends on board. None knew if they would ever see them again.

"You Must Get In at Once!"

As time passed, it became increasingly obvious that the ship would soon sink—probably before help arrived. After 1 A.M., crew members became less patient with those who hesitated. "I don't want to go in that boat!" [13] one woman cried, but a crewman seized her and dumped her into a lifeboat anyhow. First-class passenger Molly Brown received the same treatment. In their zeal to fill one of the last lifeboats, Second Officer Robert Lightoller and other crewmen started passing women through the open windows of the ship and into the boat as it hung outside.

Others implored those remaining, especially the women, to leave while they still could. "Ladies, you must get in at once!" called out Thomas Andrews, who had directed the building of the *Titanic* and was on the voyage to make a last inspection of his men's handiwork. "You cannot pick and choose your boat. Don't hesitate. Get in. Get in!" [14]

Some continued to hang back, either resigned to their fate or insistent that they would not go without husbands or other family members. By this time, though, nearly every passenger on board was aware of the danger. The aimless wandering on the deck had ceased. With or without their valuables,

The Unsinkable Molly Brown

Molly Brown was one of the most interesting people to escape from the *Titanic*. A millionaire who lived in Colorado, Brown ended up in a lifeboat commanded by crew member Robert Hichens. The men had difficulty rowing, and Brown decided that she and another woman would help out. At that point, the boat began to move quickly away from the sinking ship.

Hichens quickly grew pessimistic about their chances of escape. He was certain that the sinking ship would pull their boat underneath. Even after the *Titanic* was gone, he persisted in thinking that they would all die. After a while he decided that the people in the boat should stop rowing and let their craft drift instead. Brown, however, objected strenuously. She pointed out that those who rowed were better able to keep themselves warm.

When Hichens refused to permit her to row further, she seized her oar anyway and threatened to throw Hichens overboard if he did not give in. Hichens swore at her, but she paid him no heed. Near dawn the group made it safely to the *Carpathia*, assisted in part by the able rowing of Brown and another woman on board the boat.

Brown's exploits became well known. Her adventures helped win her entry into fashionable Denver society, and she nearly won a seat in Congress in 1914. After her death, her life became the subject of a Broadway musical called *The Unsinkable Molly Brown*.

Molly Brown helped row her lifeboat to safety after the Titanic *sank.*

with or without their families, dozens of people hurried to the nearest lifeboats and tried to climb in.

Unfortunately, by this time, most of the lifeboats had already left. And those remaining were already filled to capacity. For many stragglers, there was simply no room. Desperate passengers, realizing that they would die if they did not manage to board a lifeboat, ran frantically across the ship's tilted deck in search of an empty seat, or tried to push their way onto boats filled past capacity.

The End of the *Titanic*

Others found more complicated ways of reaching safety. From their vantage point at the end of the deck, Hugh Woolner and Bjornstrom Steffanson noticed several empty seats in a lifeboat just being lowered. Woolner quickly leaped into the bow, or front, of the lifeboat. Steffanson tried jumping, too, but bounced off the edge of the boat; Woolner pulled him in just before the boat hit the water. Both survived.

Two crew members found an even more dangerous way into one of the boats: they climbed down the ropes as it prepared to cast off from the *Titanic*.

And several parents, recognizing that they had no chance of escaping the disaster, literally tossed their children into overfilled lifeboats. "Look after this, will you?" someone shouted to Violet Jessop, throwing what looked like a package in her direction. "I reached out," she recalled later, "to receive someone's forgotten baby in my arms."[15]

Shortly before 2:00 on the morning of April 15, the last of the sixteen lifeboats cast off from the sinking *Titanic*. One of the four collapsible boats had already been loaded with passengers and set loose in the ocean.

Passengers in lifeboats watch as the Titanic's *stern slips beneath the water only minutes after the ship broke in two.*

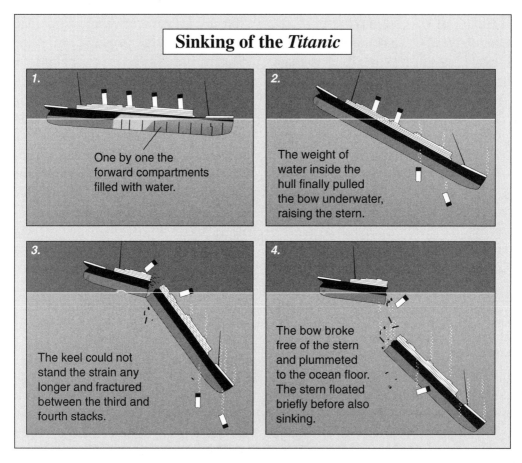

Sinking of the *Titanic*

1. One by one the forward compartments filled with water.

2. The weight of water inside the hull finally pulled the bow underwater, raising the stern.

3. The keel could not stand the strain any longer and fractured between the third and fourth stacks.

4. The bow broke free of the stern and plummeted to the ocean floor. The stern floated briefly before also sinking.

A few minutes after the departure of the final lifeboat, a second collapsible was launched as well. Second Officer Robert Lightoller and several other crew members struggled to prepare the last two collapsibles. Although they could not begin to rescue all fifteen hundred people remaining aboard the ship, Lightoller hoped to take at least a few more out of harm's way.

But it was too late. The bow of the mighty ship had sunk below the water. The deck reached an angle so sharp that people began sliding into the ocean below. A gigantic wave swept across what remained of the *Titanic*, washing the collapsibles into the Atlantic. As the people in the lifeboats watched in horror and fascination, the majestic ship then split in two. Within a matter of minutes, perhaps less, both halves had plunged below the surface. The *Titanic* was gone.

Robert Lightoller and the Collapsible Boat

Most of the people still on the ship as it actually sank were thrown into the bitter waters of the Atlantic, where they slowly froze to death. The temperature of the water simply did not permit survival, in most cases, past ten or twenty minutes. The cries of the dying, remembered one passenger, formed "one continuous wailing chant . . . like locusts on a midsummer night."[16] But even at this late moment, a small number of passengers and crewmen managed to escape.

Robert Lightoller, for instance, dived into the water as the ship began to plummet. The sensation of the frigid water against his skin, he said later, felt like "a thousand knives"[17]; still, he started to swim his way clear of the sinking ship. Unfortunately, currents created by the sinking ship quickly pulled him under the water. A Christian Scientist, Lightoller turned to his faith for comfort and support. "Let's see if Christian Science really works,"[18] he murmured as he vainly tried to kick himself free.

Escape, Controversy, and Sir Cosmo

British lord Sir Cosmo Duff Gordon and his wife Lucile left the *Titanic* on a lifeboat that carried only twelve people, seven of them crewmen. Several days after the sinking of the ship, one of those crewmen made a shocking claim. As the ship began to sink, he said, he had suggested rowing back toward it to pick up as many victims as possible. But Sir Cosmo, the crewman charged, had refused—and had offered the crewmen aboard the lifeboat five pounds each if they would stay away.

There was no doubt that Sir Cosmo had offered money to the men; he had given them written promises to that effect. But Sir Cosmo quickly denied that the money was a bribe. On the contrary, he said, he had offered them cash out of sheer generosity. After all, he pointed out, the men were now out of a job. And Sir Cosmo flatly denied that any discussion of going back to help others had ever taken place.

But many people did not find Sir Cosmo's explanation convincing. Appearing at an inquiry into the causes of the sinking, Sir Cosmo was asked whether it had occurred to him that he might have been able to help. His answers were vague and contradictory, as quoted in Don Lynch and Ken Marschall's book, *Titanic: An Illustrated History*. "There were many things to think about," he said at one point, "but of course it quite well occurred to one that people in the water might be saved by a boat." Later in the hearing, though, he insisted that "the possibility of being able to help anybody never occurred to me at all."

No one ever proved that Sir Cosmo had bribed the crewmen not to go back. And even if he had consciously rejected the idea of returning to help other victims, he would not have been alone: Sadly, most of the boats stayed away. Still, Sir Cosmo's boat was nearly empty, and both the Duff Gordons were celebrities; more was expected from them. A contemporary poem asked pointedly if Sir Cosmo had behaved "as a gentleman or [as] a coward," and plenty of observers chose the latter. Neither Sir Cosmo nor Lucile ever quite regained their good names in the wake of the *Titanic* disaster.

Whether it was faith or coincidence, Lightoller's time had not yet come. A blast of heat from a ventilator shaft pushed him back up to the surface. Gasping for breath, Lightoller looked up and saw one of the last two collapsibles. Lightoller swam to it, seized a piece of rope attached to the boat, and climbed on. The boat had washed out of the *Titanic* in an upside-down position, but it was a great deal better than nothing.

Even so, Lightoller was scarcely in a safe place. The sinking ship was nearly on top of him, and the collapsible could offer no protection against the whirling currents. Once again, Lightoller prepared for death. But once again, he was in luck. A piece of one of the *Titanic*'s smokestacks fell off and landed directly behind him. The resulting wave carried Lightoller and his improvised craft out of harm's way.

Lightoller was not the only person who found refuge on the collapsible. Passenger Jack Thayer had jumped into the water from a rail of the sinking ship, a distance he would later estimate as about thirty feet. Eager to avoid the currents that had sucked Lightoller down with the ship, Thayer swam underwater as far as he could. When he looked up, he too was thrilled to see the collapsible nearby. Swimming over, he joined Lightoller.

Although the collapsible was the wrong way up and partly filled with water, it nevertheless became the only hope for almost thirty people who had fled the ship at the last possible minute. Some had left the ship clutching the collapsible. But most, like Thayer and Lightoller, had reached it from the water. This group included a ship's fireman who had badly burned his hands earlier that evening; an American military officer; and Rosa Abbott, a third-class passenger thrown into the sea when the ship went down. Later, they would meet up with another lifeboat and clamber aboard, abandoning the collapsible.

Rescue

Simply finding refuge aboard a lifeboat did not guarantee a safe escape. Exposed as they were to the elements, several of the people who had escaped the wreck died that night, including two anonymous crewmen crammed atop Lightoller's collapsible. And the remaining survivors found themselves losing hope as the night went on. A few of the passengers and crew began to fear the worst. "This is no joke," one crew member told others in his boat. "We may knock around here days before we are picked up, if at all."[19]

In fact, the steamer *Carpathia* had heard the *Titanic*'s signal of distress. At about 4:00 that morning, it hurried into the area. The appearance of the ship on the distant horizon revived hope again. "Many among those poor weeping, frozen people, murmuring prayers in a soft monotone," recalled Violet Jessop, "nearly died with emotion when they sighted that ship."[20] Slowly, the men and

More than ninety years after the disaster, the remains of the Titanic *still rest on the ocean floor.*

women in the lifeboats and the collapsibles made their way to the *Carpathia*'s side, where they were taken aboard and given food, water, and medical attention. In all, just over 700 of the original 2,201 survived.

Their experience had been grueling. They were cold, wet, and frightened. Many had lost parents, spouses, children, or friends aboard the sunken vessel. But they were safe. They had successfully escaped from the sinking *Titanic*.

2

Escape from Bhopal

ON THE NIGHT of December 3, 1984, a devastating industrial accident took place in the city of Bhopal, India. As most of the city's seven hundred thousand residents slept, an extremely toxic chemical known as methyl isocyanate, or MIC, began to leak from the storage tanks of a pesticide factory located on the outskirts of town. Before the factory workers could close the leak, deadly gas spilled into the air surrounding the factory. Quickly, the gas began to spread toward the unsuspecting citizens sleeping nearby.

For those Bhopal residents who were directly downwind of the leak, the results were horrifying. MIC is an extraordinarily dangerous substance with a host of negative effects on the human body, most notably on the eyes and on

the respiratory system. In particular, MIC puts the throat and airways into spasms, preventing air from getting through to the lungs. "You can compare [the effects of MIC exposure] to a very dramatic asthma attack,"[21] says a scientist who has studied the substance. Even in small doses, MIC is a killer. Thousands of Bhopal residents died as a result of its accidental release.

But despite the gas's virulent effects, most residents of Bhopal managed to escape death that night. Even in the areas most seriously affected by the release of MIC, a majority survived. Some stayed in their houses, breathing shallowly to avoid being overcome by the deadly chemical. Others ran ahead of the approaching gas, and still others climbed aboard scooters, trucks, and

28

cars; some piled onto vehicles' fenders and roofs in an effort to escape the poisonous cloud. What happened at Bhopal is known today as the world's worst industrial accident. It would have been far more deadly, however, if not for the quick action of thousands of the city's residents.

Pesticides, India, and Union Carbide

In 1969, an American chemical company called Union Carbide built a pesticide manufacturing plant just outside Bhopal, in the central Indian state of Madhya Pradesh. Union Carbide anticipated a burgeoning market for pesticides in heavily agricultural India and hoped that the Bhopal factory could meet the expected demand. By 1984, the plant was producing several thousand tons of pesticides annually.

From its beginnings, the plant was a fixture in Bhopal. It was a source of pride among residents of the city. Run mainly by native-born Indians, the factory seemed a visible sign of modernity and progress. Bhopal's citizens knew, too, that the pesticides the plant churned out played a role in increasing India's food supply and productivity. The factory attracted some of India's brightest and most ambitious engineers and managers, who were lured in part by the unusually high wages paid by Union Carbide.

The Shantytowns of Bhopal

When Union Carbide constructed the Bhopal factory, few people lived in the surrounding area. But over the years, the city had expanded considerably, both in area and in population. By 1984, an estimated one hundred thousand people lived in several neighborhoods just south and east of the factory's gates. Most of these areas were shantytowns, home to some of the region's poorest people. These men, women, and children lived in tumbledown shacks, mostly made of mud, wood, or metal. Nearly all the homes in these parts of town lacked electricity and running water, and many had no solid doors or windows.

The toxins would have had a terrible impact on any section of Bhopal, but the effect on these neighborhoods was especially dramatic. This area of Bhopal was thickly populated, so the gas affected many more people than it might have in less densely settled parts of town. Moreover, the shoddy construction of the shantytowns made the residents of these neighborhoods particularly vulnerable to the toxic fumes. Strong brick walls and sturdy roofs might have prevented some of the lethal gases from entering, but the citizens of the shantytowns did not have such luxuries. While exact figures are lacking, most observers agree that the death rate in the poorest areas of Bhopal was considerably higher than the death rate in wealthier areas affected by the cloud.

In the late 1960s, the American chemical company Union Carbide built a pesticide manufacturing plant, like this one, outside the Indian city of Bhopal.

Unfortunately, the factory's presence in Bhopal was a mixed blessing. Pesticide production requires technicians to work with a variety of extremely hazardous substances, and the Bhopal facility had no shortage of deadly chemicals. Of these, probably the most lethal was MIC, which is a mix of carbon, nitrogen, and several other elements. MIC was an essential ingredient in manufacturing a Union Carbide pesticide named Sevin. It is also extremely deadly. Even in tiny amounts, it can kill or otherwise harm human beings. Indeed, for many years after MIC's use in pesticide production was discovered, the chemical was so dangerous that few researchers dared to study it closely.

The people who ran Union Carbide's Bhopal plant were well aware of the dangers posed by MIC. The company warned workers that the substance was extremely deadly and needed to be handled with the utmost care. Since it was easier to contain MIC as a liquid than a gas, regulations required that it be stored as a liquid. Similarly, the rules called for employees to wear masks and protective clothing while working with the chemical. "Stringent precautions must be observed to eliminate any possibility of human contact,"[22] summed up a Union Carbide manual used at the Indian plant.

Despite the safety procedures, however, accidents did happen. In 1978, for instance, a fire broke out in an area of the factory where chemicals were stored. "Nobody in Bhopal slept that night,"[23] remembered a local resident several years later. In 1981, a worker died when he accidentally inhaled a deadly chemical produced at the plant. One year later, a trace of MIC somehow leaked from a storage tank, sending one worker to the hospital. And small amounts of MIC were found to be leaking on at least one other occasion as well.

Publicly, factory officials stated that these safety lapses were isolated incidents. Some, they argued, were preventable accidents, caused by workers who ignored the procedures they had been taught. Others were no one's fault: they were the natural result of running a factory that dealt with toxic substances. There was some truth to both statements. However, there was a good deal more to the story.

A Worsening Situation

The truth was, by the early 1980s, the managers of the Bhopal factory had stopped keeping a close eye on safety. The reason was financial: Indian farmers were not buying Union Carbide pesticides at the rate company officials had expected. In an effort to save money, Union Carbide officials lowered production considerably at the Bhopal facility. They also cut the factory's workforce by about a third. Both moves did indeed reduce the financial losses faced by the company.

The company's managers also began to cut corners in training, preventive maintenance, and other essential areas. "A pipe leaked?" summarized writer

Dan Kurzman, who talked to many of the plant's workers following the disaster. "Don't replace it, employees said they were told. Just patch it up."[24] According to Kurzman, conversations of this sort were frequent in the early 1980s, though plant officials hotly disputed that instructions of this sort came from them.

Wherever the blame lay, there was little doubt that the Bhopal plant did not stress safety as much as it should have. In 1982, an inspection team from a Union Carbide manufacturing plant in West Virginia arrived at the factory. Part of the team's purpose was to look for safety violations, and the team members found dozens. The factory, they charged, was "strewn with oily old drums, used piping, pools of used oil and chemical waste likely to cause fire."[25] Their report went on to cite more than sixty other violations at the plant, among them rusted valves, missing gauges, and backup safety equipment that had not been tested, in some cases, for over a year.

But the report resulted in little more than cosmetic changes. Evidently, no one from company headquarters made sure the inspectors' recommendations were followed. Other than pointing out problems, Union Carbide officials seemed to pay little attention to what was going on in Bhopal. That mindset would eventually lead to tragedy.

A Leak

On the evening of December 2, 1984, a supervisor at the Bhopal plant ordered a worker to clean out several drainpipes connected to the MIC tanks. In following his instructions, the worker noticed that a small disk called a slip blind was missing from one of the pipes. The slip blind was designed to prevent water from flowing into the MIC tanks and possibly causing a violent reaction. According to the company manuals, missing slip blinds were supposed to be replaced immediately. But the worker did not do so; the evidence suggests that he was unaware of the requirement.

The mistake would prove lethal. Shortly before midnight, workers in the control room realized that pressure was building inside one of the MIC storage tanks. Around the same time, an employee noticed that his eyes seemed somewhat irritated—a possible indicator of a tiny MIC leak somewhere in the plant. Neither event was exceptionally unusual; nor was either, in itself, especially dangerous. Minuscule amounts of MIC had leaked out into the factory before, after all, and the pressure gauges on the tanks had never been completely reliable. "It's your dial that's gone mad,"[26] supervisor Shekil Qureshi assured a concerned employee.

Qureshi's words were comforting. Nevertheless, several workers did investigate the MIC area, where they were dismayed to find a small amount of liquid, probably MIC, dripping slowly from an overhead pipe. At the same time, employees in the control room noticed that the pressure and temperature gauges on the tanks were climbing

Rusted and leaking barrels filled with toxic chemicals were one of many hazards at the Bhopal factory.

dangerously high. Now Qureshi, too, was alarmed. Fearing that the situation was out of control, he ordered an employee to broadcast an alert over the plant's internal loudspeaker.

Disaster

As investigators later reconstructed the event, the lack of the slip blind had indeed allowed trickles of water to filter through the drainpipe and into the MIC tanks. There it reacted with the MIC, creating heat and turning much of the toxic liquid into equally toxic gas. With the higher temperatures came greater pressure, forcing the MIC to expand. Some of what remained in liquid form was squeezed into the pipes and out weak areas in the transporting system; it was this that the employees had seen dripping onto the floor in the MIC storage area.

The MIC gas, however, did not follow the path of the liquid. Instead, it popped open a closed safety valve and shot into an emergency vent pipe leading to the

As the factory's backup safety systems failed, toxic gas like this began to fill the air above the Bhopal factory.

outside. In theory, at this point the disaster could still have been averted. On its way out of the factory, the gas had to pass through a scrubber designed to bombard the escaping MIC with a neutralizing chemical. Unfortunately, like so much else in the factory, the scrubber was not functioning properly. And even if it had been in perfect working order, the MIC's volume and temperature would probably have been too much for the neutralizing agent.

The workers did not yet panic. The factory had been equipped with several other backup safety devices to ensure that the MIC did not escape from the proper tanks. But the men's concern grew steadily as one by one, each of the backup systems failed to work any better than the scrubber. A series of water jets proved too weak to overwhelm the escaping gas. A pipeline designed to burn the MIC was too badly rusted to be used. And a backup refrigeration system, intended to help bring down the tank's temperature and convert the gas back into liquid form, had been taken out of service. "The refrigerant, Freon 22, had been removed for utilisation elsewhere," explained one person familiar with the plant's operation. "[The system] couldn't have been started for hours."[27]

Shortly after midnight on December 3, it became evident to everyone in the factory that they had run out of options.

MIC was pouring into the atmosphere around the plant at an alarming rate. There was nothing more that anyone could do to stop the poisonous vapors from escaping into the surrounding area. "Give the order for everyone to evacuate," Qureshi directed his assistant, "and let's get out of here!"[28]

The Escape of Shekil Qureshi

For the most part, those inside the factory at the time of the gas leak were only mildly affected by the poison. One employee checked the wind direction before the workers fled the plant and directed the group to head north, away from the worst of the cloud. Moreover, most of the men in the plant followed safety procedures for an orderly evacuation, which included putting on gas masks and portable oxygen tanks. The combination assisted them in reaching safety without succumbing to the poisons.

Shekil Qureshi, the supervisor, was not so fortunate. After giving the order to evacuate, he discovered that his own mask and oxygen tank were missing. (What had happened to them remains a mystery.) As the toxic chemical MIC swirled toward him, Qureshi had no time to search for replacements. Instead, he took a deep breath, put his head down, and ran. Overweight and out of shape, Qureshi was in no condition to exert himself, but these were not ordinary circumstances. "I was so afraid of dying," he told Dominique Lapierre and Javier Moro, as quoted in their book *Five Past Midnight in Bhopal*, "I felt capable of anything."

Qureshi hurried to the nearest exit and dashed out of the factory. He found little relief outside, however. Toxic gas covered the courtyard between the plant and the neighborhoods of Bhopal. Choking and nearly blinded, Qureshi struggled onward toward the six-foot-high security fence that surrounded the factory. Somehow he clambered up to the top of the fence, where he gingerly made his way across the barbed wire stretched along the edge. Then, trying to maneuver himself to drop safely down the other side, he lost his balance and fell, breaking a leg.

Still Qureshi did not give up. He dragged himself forward to a leaky fire hydrant and positioned his body so it would catch the running water. Then he pulled off his shirt, soaked it in the moisture, and held it up to his mouth and nose. This strategy, which filtered out some of the poison before it entered his lungs, could not keep the supervisor conscious, but it did keep him alive. Rescuers found him later that morning and brought him to a hospital. Though his lung capacity was permanently compromised, Qureshi survived.

"It Was Like Breathing Fire"

Under different weather conditions, the MIC gas might have posed little danger to the people of the neighborhoods surrounding the factory. Southerly winds might have blown the worst of the vapors away from the settled areas of Bhopal. Some experts believe that hot weather that evening might have helped disperse the gas. But the early morning of December 3 was cool, misty, and calm. The combination kept the poison heavily concentrated and low to the ground. Quickly, poison spilled from the factory vents and began to spread toward the nearby residential areas.

Soon after midnight on December 3, thousands of Bhopal residents were shaken from their sleep by a terrible pain settling mainly in their eyes, throats, and chests. Choking and coughing, they gasped for air. "It was both a burning and a suffocating situation," recalled one man who received a dangerous dose of the MIC. "It was like breathing fire."[29]

Residents of the affected areas hurriedly fled their homes and streamed into the streets. Those who could went from house to house alerting still-sleeping friends and neighbors to the situation. A few held cloths over their faces to assist them in breathing; others covered their eyes, itchy and tearing from the effects of the MIC. But while these measures alleviated some of the worst effects of the gas, they scarcely eliminated the danger.

To make matters worse, very few Bhopal residents initially had any idea what was going on. Although MIC has a distinctive odor and a whitish yellow color, not everyone immediately made the connection between the gas and the nearby chemical factory. That was especially true because factory workers did not set off the plant's emergency siren until well after the gas had escaped. As a result, most people did not suspect a chemical leak. "I thought it was a plague,"[30] recalled one man. Others assumed the gas was the result of a terrorist attack, fire, or even a train wreck.

Whatever the cause, it was clear that something had gone horribly wrong. Thousands of Bhopal residents struggled to draw breath, their voices raspy and weak by the effects of the gas. For many, vision had suddenly become limited or nonexistent; one resident recalled that his eyes were as painful "as if someone had flung chillies into a fire."[31] Fearing for their lives, the people of the affected neighborhoods frantically began to search for refuge.

Staying Put

For many people, the safest option proved to be remaining where they were. This choice, while counterintuitive to some, did make a certain amount of sense. In the chaos, many people who chose flight unwittingly headed into areas where the gas was even stronger. Moreover, the physical activity of flight, by increasing the need for air, actually drove more of the poisonous chemical

Animals killed by the poisonous gas litter a street in Bhopal. Although many people and animals died in the disaster, thousands survived.

into the lungs. Although exact figures are lacking, some observers believe that the death rate was significantly lower among those who chose to remain where they were than among those who decided to flee.

That was especially true in the wealthier areas affected by the cloud of MIC. Sturdy brick houses and public buildings, common in these parts of town, kept out the worst of the gas: these structures had solid walls, along with tight-fitting doors and windows, making it more difficult for the poison to seep inside. One well-off citizen near the factory simply closed an open window when he saw gas creeping in. After that, he stayed where he was until the poison began to dissipate. In the end, he escaped the disaster unhurt.

The situation was not so favorable in the poorer sections of the city. Ramshackle houses did not keep out the toxins as effectively as sturdier dwellings. Gas slipped between the planks of shoddily constructed wooden walls and wafted through the open doorways of mud huts. Still, many of Bhopal's poorest residents did their best to outlast the lethal cloud. Lying still and breathing through wet cloths (which helps to filter out dangerous particles), they managed to survive the worst of the disaster.

Remaining in place was far from easy, both physically and emotionally. Many of those who chose to stay, especially those in the poorest areas of the city, had experiences similar to those of Baba Lakkad Das, an elderly

The Train Station

One of the most dramatic incidents during the Bhopal disaster took place at the local train station, which lay directly in the path of the worst of the gas. A busy place at all hours of the day and night, the open-air platforms were full of people even after midnight on a Monday morning; by some estimates, as many as six hundred were milling around the station when the MIC began to leak. Rail travel is popular in India, and several trains were due in at Bhopal that night. Among those scheduled was the Bombay–Gorakhpur Express, expected to arrive shortly before 1 A.M.

A few minutes before the express appeared, the MIC cloud hit the railroad station. Members of the crowd succumbed quickly to the toxins. The attack was sudden and swift. Within seconds, most of the people at the station were writhing on the ground, gasping for air. For most, there was no refuge, and no chance of rescue. Other than a handful of railroad workers in an office at one end of the platform, few at the station that night survived the ordeal.

One of the survivors was railroad official V.K. Sharma. Watching in horror from his desk in the control office, Sharma knew he could do little for the victims outside. Instead, he turned his attention to the express train due to pull into the station at any minute. Sharma had no idea what was causing this deadly cloud, but he could easily imagine the consequences if the train stopped to discharge passengers: not only would all those disembarking be walking into the worst of the poison, but an influx of the gas would sweep onto the train and kill most of those who remained on board.

As the train glided to a stop in the Bhopal station, Sharma did the only thing he could. Ignoring the risk to himself, he ran forward and waved frantically at the engineer. As the doors opened, he urged the crew to leave immediately without discharging any passengers. The engineer asked no questions. Although a handful of passengers did get off, the doors quickly closed behind them and the train sped off into the night. Sharma's heroism had saved countless lives.

man living in one of the most impoverished parts of Bhopal. After deciding to stay put, Das focused most of his energy on simply staying alive. "He couldn't open his eyes," wrote one reporter about Das's ordeal. "He could barely breathe. And the pain in his stomach was unbearable."[32] Eventually, he was rendered unconscious by the gas. But the chemicals did not kill him.

Nor did they kill thousands of others who, like Das, decided to stay where they were.

Bhopal's Hiroshima

But although many people did survive by staying where they were, remaining in place simply did not seem to be an option for thousands of others. These people obeyed their first impulse: to flee. Most left their homes and struggled out into the night with nothing more than what was on their backs. Few took the time to bring along more than a handful of easily reached mementos and other valuables, though a moneylender named Pulpul Singh loaded an entire safe into a cart before hurrying off.

Eyewitnesses later reported that the chaos on the streets was astonishing. People stumbled blindly among the houses, calling for family members. Some could not see at all; others had limited vision at best. The lucky ones were found and assisted in their escape by those less immediately affected by the poison. In the confusion, families became separated—children slipped from their parents' grasp and husbands and wives lost track of each other's whereabouts.

Television repairman Sayed Abbas was one of many who became disoriented as a result of the gas. Abbas tried to borrow or commandeer a vehicle to help move his family to safety, but he met with no success. Worse, the farther he ran, the more the gas affected his eyes. At some point Abbas realized that he no longer knew where he was. With no chance of finding his way back to his family, Abbas would have to find a way to escape on his own.

Many of the victims simply headed into the night, rushing in any direction in hopes of escaping the gas. But others took the time to work out a plan. Some of Bhopal's poorest residents, for instance, hurried to the nearest brick

buildings. Knowing or suspecting that the stronger construction would limit their exposure, they banged on the doors of the closest private houses. Frightened, some of the homeowners insisted that the refugees leave immediately. Others, in contrast, welcomed them in. Omar Pasha, a wealthy resident in one poor neighborhood, allowed dozens of people to seek shelter inside his two-story home. He and his servants provided food and water, handed out wet cloths to cool victims' eyes, and did their best to care for those who had already been affected by the gas. With his help, many of these refugees survived.

Others raced to hospitals, partly for the possibility of medical assistance—but also in hopes that a large public building might provide shelter. Hundreds of survivors ran in the general direction of Hamidia Hospital, just outside the affected area, where medical staff quickly set up a field hospital in addition to the regular facilities. Refugees from the cloud sped to the gates of the hospital, some of them coughing up blood, others in intense pain from the gas's effect on the eyes. Surveying the scene, one doctor was reminded of the atomic bomb dropped on Hiroshima, Japan, at the end of World War II. "Tonight," he thought, surveying the anguished crowds in need of medical attention, "the Bhopalis are going through their Hiroshima."[33]

Others tried to escape by outrunning the poison. Checking the direction in which the lethal cloud was traveling, these people tried to determine the quickest route out from its influence. Some headed north and east, others more directly west; it all depended on where they were and which direction seemed more promising. Some guessed wrong. Blundering into areas where the gases were even stronger, they fell dead by the roadside.

But many others guessed right. As they hurried along, often dragging children or blinded adults by the hand, they found that the intensity of the gas gradually lessened. Some came to a stop outside Bhopal's largest mosque, where a pool of water helped soothe burned throats and tearing eyes. Others hastened to the countryside just beyond the city limits. These and other lucky survivors found a route that eventually took them beyond the influence of the gas.

Escaping on Foot

The journey of these survivors was harrowing. Most of the affected had to rely on their own strength and ingenuity in making their escapes. While emergency services personnel responded to the tragedy as soon as they learned of it, the failure of the factory alarm to sound had cost

them precious minutes. And the level of support, in any case, did not approach the need. Public transportation officials hastily put the city's bus fleet into service, for example, but the city owned too few buses to evacuate more than a handful of victims.

With no organized evacuation plans, most residents of Bhopal were left to head to safety in any way they could. As Sayed Abbas realized, cars and oth-

Survivors identify bodies outside Hamidia Hospital. During the disaster, many city residents crowded into the hospital.

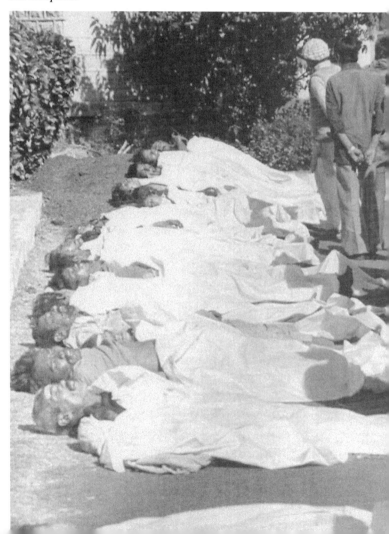

Refugees escape the Bhopal disaster on foot. Many residents, especially those from poor neighborhoods, escaped the disaster on foot.

er motor vehicles were hard to find in poorer areas, so most refugees traveled on foot. Most had at least two miles to go before they could be truly safe. The victims picked their way through the deadly cloud as best they could, choking, rubbing their eyes, and occasionally vomiting from the effects of the gas.

For most, progress was agonizingly slow. Men dragged along pregnant wives; parents carried two or even three children at a time. Those who could see led blinded relatives through the crowded streets. "It was Kafkaesque that night," remembered a politician, likening the situation to the distorted and surreal works of the Austrian writer Franz Kafka. "People running all over . . . shards of glass on the road."[34]

Some of the refugees, unable to reach safety before the gas overcame their lungs, collapsed as they hurried forward. A few somehow managed to survive the experience. Some were brought to hospitals later that morning and were given appropriate medical care. Sayed Abbas, who was overcome by fumes while trying to escape along a railroad track, was found by rescuers but was at first believed to be dead. He was carried to the morgue, where he lay unconscious for a few hours. Then, suddenly, he awakened. He eventually got up and left the morgue.

Others who tried to escape on foot reached safety on their own. Despite a painful burning sensation in his eyes,

This photo captures the chaotic scene at Bhopal's train station as residents fled the city the day after the gas leak.

metalworker Sayed Khan successfully fled his shantytown neighborhood just outside the factory gates. A pregnant woman not only survived the two-mile trek to the edge of town, but gave birth to a baby a few hours afterward. Their experiences were not unusual among those who set out to walk, run, or stumble away from the contaminated air.

Vehicles

While most of the poor struggled along on foot, luckier—and often wealthier—residents of Bhopal made use of other methods. Some had scooters or bicycles, which made progress quicker. Others had cars, vans, or small three-wheeled motorized vehicles. Under ideal circumstances, the owners of these vehicles could escape in much less time than those forced to rely on their feet.

Maneuvering a vehicle through the crowded streets of Bhopal was difficult under normal conditions, and was almost impossible in the wake of the gas leak. The roads were clogged with thousands of frantic people—many unable to see—as well as corpses of people and animals. Moreover, the gas irritated the drivers' own eyes, thereby limiting their vision. Accidents were common.

Still, there is no doubt that people with access to vehicles were more likely to escape than those without. "They were in tempos [small vans], in buses," recalled M.N. Nagoo, the director of Bhopal's health services. "Anything that could get them away from the factory."[35] Journalist Rajkumar Keswani and his family successfully fled from the cloud on the household's two motor scooters. L.S. Loya, the staff physician at the Union Carbide plant, ferried several relatives to safety on his own motor scooter, then returned to the affected area to lend medical assistance.

Many drivers were stopped by desperate Bhopalis, who pleaded for a ride or simply jumped into passing vehicles. Sharda Diwedi, an official at the local power plant, said later that several dozen people had tried to climb into his Jeep as he drove toward safety. About forty more attempted to climb onto the car being driven by Nagoo. In both cases, terrified residents nestled on the roof, clung to the doors, and jammed inside the trunk. Neither Diwedi nor Nagoo could carry all those clamoring for a ride; still, each drove off with as many passengers as his car could manage.

Some drivers, too, volunteered their services to other needy passengers. Timothy Wankhede, an Anglican minister, was awakened that morning by the screams of his baby son. Believing that there was no escape, he brought his wife and son into his church, where he and his wife prayed and awaited death. But a passing driver pulled up outside the building to check on Wankhede on his way out of town. Although his car already had several passengers, he made room for the Wankhedes. All three survived.

Courage, Resourcefulness, and Luck

The storage tank in the Union Carbide factory was empty by 3 A.M. and the cloud of toxic MIC finally dissipated shortly before dawn. It left in its wake thousands of corpses, and many more slowly dying. Estimates of the death toll range from an official tally of thirty-five hundred up to almost ten times that number, with most who have studied the issue assuming a minimum figure of eight thousand. There is no question that the cloud was a killer.

Even some of the escapes were bittersweet. While fleeing from the city into the safety of nearby farmland, a ten-year-old boy known only as Zahir was separated from his parents, who were later presumed to be dead. Sayed Khan, the metalworker, lost at least four family members in the disaster. Another man found only one of his four children still alive.

Others survived, only to find that the effects of MIC did not vanish as quickly as the gas. Though most who had been blinded that night would recover some of their vision, some continued to have trouble with their eyes. Similarly,

Many Bhopal residents suffered severe injuries as a result of the disaster. Toxic gas blinded this woman.

exposure to MIC resulted in permanent damage to the lungs and throats of many who escaped death. Even today, the residual health consequences of the poisoning are a significant problem in Bhopal.

The suffering of the people of Bhopal cannot be minimized. The early morning of December 3 brought terror to the city far outweighing that of most other man-made disasters throughout history. Still, what is remarkable about Bhopal is not the number who died, but the number who survived. Despite the horrific effects of the toxins, hundreds of thousands of people lived through the night—and beyond. They did not give in, they did not lose hope. Through courage, resourcefulness, and luck, they escaped death.

3

Escape from the *Hindenburg*

THE CRASH OF a large passenger aircraft is among the most tragic of all man-made disasters. Though such crashes seldom occur, they usually result in extremely high death tolls. It is not uncommon for an air wreck to result in the death of everyone on board. The combination of an aircraft's speed and altitude, and the cramped design of an airplane cabin, work together to make escape from an air crash difficult, if not impossible.

Still, death sentences from an air crash are not necessarily a certainty. Again and again in the history of aviation, crew members and passengers have successfully escaped air wrecks that seemed certain to take the lives of everyone on board. Through ingenuity and thoughtfulness, and motivated in

part by plain everyday fear, some of the victims of these crashes walk away from the scene alive—and, in some cases, scarcely injured.

Most modern examples of these escapes involve airplanes. But perhaps the most remarkable escape from an aircraft disaster involves a different kind of flying machine altogether. In 1937, the *Hindenburg*, a rigid airship known as a zeppelin or dirigible, caught on fire as it approached a landing pad in Lakehurst, New Jersey. Within seconds, the entire airship had burned to an unrecognizable skeleton as onlookers watched in horror—and as a radio reporter frantically described the scene to listeners all across America.

The crash of the *Hindenburg* would become known as perhaps the most

The Hindenburg *bursts into flames and crashes in May 1937. Surprisingly, most of the passengers and crew survived the disaster.*

famous man-made disaster to take place in America in the 1930s. Yet sixty-two of the ninety-seven people on board the *Hindenburg* that day survived, many of them with only minor injuries. How these men, women, and children made their way out of the falling, burning zeppelin makes for one of the more dramatic escape stories in history.

The Airships of Ferdinand von Zeppelin

Invented by and named for Ferdinand von Zeppelin, a German count with a strong interest in aerodynamics, the zeppelin was an early alternative to the airplane. Zeppelins were wingless, long, and vaguely cylindrical, much like present-day blimps. Although zeppelins carried engines, mechanical equipment, and compartments for cargo and passengers, the great bulk of each craft was a rigid shell, sometimes known as the skin, held in place by a metal frame and divided into chambers, or cells. Each cell could be filled with a lighter-than-air gas. If enough cells were filled, a zeppelin would slowly rise into the atmosphere in the same way that a helium-filled toy balloon, once released, will float into the sky.

Bringing the airship back to Earth was more complicated. But the general principle was simple enough: if gas made the zeppelin rise, then removing the gas would cause it to sink. Count Zeppelin devised a system of valves that could release specified amounts of the gas on demand. Like hot air balloons, zeppelins carried ballast, or extra weight, mostly in the form of water. By shifting the location of the weight, or releasing it altogether, a pilot could change the altitude and angle at which he flew.

Riding in a zeppelin was quite different from being a passenger in a modern airplane. Unlike large airplanes, which usually fly several miles above the earth's surface, zeppelins typically cruised at an altitude of about eight hundred feet. Because of the low altitude, zeppelin cabins needed no pressurizing. Indeed, the windows in passenger compartments could be opened—unthinkable in one of today's jetliners.

Takeoffs and landings were also different for dirigibles. Instead of runways, they used mooring masts, tall towers to which the airships could be tied when not in use. Takeoffs were relatively straightforward; simply releasing the gas-filled airship from the mooring mast was usually enough to get it airborne. Landings were trickier. Fastening the airship to the mast required thousands of feet of ropes and wires, along with an assortment of grappling hooks. To land a large zeppelin could require a ground crew of over two hundred people.

Finally, there were important differences in speed and smoothness between zeppelins and present-day airplanes. Zeppelins moved slowly in comparison to modern planes; the most powerful zeppelins could not achieve speeds above 100 mph, and many traveled much slower than that. On the other

Count Zeppelin's Zeppelins

Ferdinand von Zeppelin was not the first to build and fly an airship that used the principle of lighter-than-air gas. By the time he made his first flight, in 1900, several other inventors had already gone aloft in crafts that looked something like overgrown hot air balloons. Nor was Zeppelin's first flight especially memorable, or noticeably superior to the earlier attempts of other aviators. Once airborne, in fact, Zeppelin discovered that his craft was neither powerful nor particularly stable. Instead, it was very much at the mercy of the wind currents. Zeppelin was lucky to keep the airship aloft for eighteen anxious minutes before bringing it down on the surface of a lake.

But Zeppelin persevered. He analyzed his design to determine which parts were successful and which ones were not, and changed his architectural plans for each succeeding model accordingly. His third machine, finished in 1906, was better than his first in every respect. His fourth made a twelve-hour nonstop flight in 1908. By this time, it was clear that Zeppelin's airships were considerably more efficient and more reliable than those of any of his competitors. It seemed entirely reasonable that the airships should be identified with him. Ever since, they have been widely known as zeppelins.

Ferdinand von Zeppelin developed the efficient airship that bears his name.

hand, zeppelins moved with such quietness and stability that passengers did not always notice that they were moving. "When are we leaving?" one airship passenger is said to have asked a steward during a flight in the 1930s. "Why madam," he responded, "we left over two hours ago."[36]

Speed, Safety, and Hydrogen Gas

As time passed, zeppelins proved themselves capable of all kinds of uses. Passenger service was first offered aboard one of Count Zeppelin's dirigibles in 1911. In 1919, several years before the first airplane would attempt the crossing, a British zeppelin made the first transatlantic dirigible flight. Seven years later, Norwegian explorer Roald Amundsen and Italian pilot Umberto Nobile flew over the North Pole in an Italian-built dirigible called the *Norge.* So impressive were the feats of the zeppelins, many people predicted that dirigibles, not airplanes, would prove to be the aircraft of the future.

While airships had many supporters, they had their disadvantages as well. Their relative lack of speed was one. Even at top speed, airships took two or three days to cross the Atlantic. In 1927, by contrast, American pilot Charles Lindbergh crossed the Atlantic in an airplane in just thirty-three hours. While airplanes were still flimsy, dangerous, and much slower than they would eventually become, they seemed even then to promise more speed than any dirigible could ever muster.

The bigger issue with zeppelins, though, was their safety record. By the 1930s, a remarkable number of dirigibles had met with disaster. Storms were one of the main culprits. Ferdinand von

Dirigibles like this one were popular during the early nineteenth century. Such airships had disadvantages, however, including slow speed and poor safety records.

Zeppelin's own LZ-4, the first airship to offer passenger service, was destroyed by violent winds while fastened to a mooring mast. In 1925, the U.S. airship *Shenandoah* broke into pieces as it flew through a thunderstorm. And in 1933, another U.S. zeppelin, the *Akron,* was also destroyed by a storm; only three of the seventy-six men on board survived.

The second safety problem with dirigibles involved the gas used to lift the machines off the ground. Zeppelins could use either hydrogen or helium to fill the interior cells. Helium was scarce and costly, and it did not have quite the lifting power of hydrogen. But hydrogen had a potentially more serious drawback: it was highly flammable. Great care had to be taken to keep the gas away from flames, sparks, or even static electricity. Several hydrogen-powered ships had burned in freak accidents. One, designed by the Italian explorer and pilot Umberto Nobile, had exploded when it was accidentally flown into a set of electric wires.

After 1921, American zeppelin builders began to move away from hydrogen in favor of helium for just this reason. Still, nearly all European zeppelins continued to use the cheaper,

The Shenandoah *lies in pieces after crashing during a 1925 storm. The* Shenandoah *was one of several airships that met with disaster in the early twentieth century.*

more plentiful hydrogen. Despite the potential dangers, few manufacturers outside the United States made the switch.

The *Hindenburg*

The acknowledged masters of the zeppelin were the Germans. Although the country's airship program had been suspended for a time following Germany's defeat in World War I, the military loss did not put a permanent end to the German interest in dirigibles. By the mid-1920s, German manufacturers were once again building the world's finest zeppelins.

Their work culminated with the completion of the *Hindenburg* in 1936. In a word, the *Hindenburg* was enormous. The ship measured 804 feet from nose to tail—and 135 feet in diameter at its widest. The sixteen gas cells contained a combined 7 million cubic feet of space. While a few earlier ships approached the size of the *Hindenburg*, no other airship could match the overall dimensions of the new German zeppelin.

Regardless of its size, the *Hindenburg* was constructed much like any other zeppelin of the time. An intricate arrangement of metal rings and crosspieces lined the interior like the spokes of a bicycle wheel, allowing the zeppelin to keep its shape even when no gas was in the cells. The rings and crosspieces, in turn, were supported by the axial corridor, a metal walkway that ran from the nose of the ship back to the tail. This corridor provided the crew with access to the gas cells. It also served to ease the stress on the rigid framework of the mighty zeppelin.

The *Hindenburg*'s control areas, too, were similar to those of other airships. The main control car was located toward the front and hung down below the cylindrical section of the ship. Further toward the back was a smaller auxiliary control room. The two were connected by a catwalk and a speaking tube, which allowed personnel to travel, and relay messages, back and forth. In good weather, automatic systems steered and controlled altitude changes. But a human operator could take over if conditions worsened.

What made the *Hindenburg* special, however, was neither the sophisticated steering system nor the strength of the rigid metal frame. Instead, it was the ship's passenger quarters. The zeppelin originally had space for about fifty passengers, all of whom traveled in comfort unknown to airplane passengers of any era. Harold G. Dick, an American who was involved in the construction of the airship, called the passenger areas "magnificent and spacious,"[37] and few passengers would have disagreed.

Indeed, the common spaces on the *Hindenburg* rivaled those of a luxury hotel. The dining room was decorated with fine art; the menus included such gourmet fare as "Fattened Duckling, Bavarian Style, with Champagne Cabbage."[38] A walkway lined with windows ran outside the cabins. A lounge near the dining room housed a grand piano; evening

The Wreck of the *Shenandoah*

Before the *Hindenburg*, one of the most dramatic survival stories involving a zeppelin had taken place in 1925. The American airship *Shenandoah* was flying over Caldwell, Ohio, that September with forty-three men aboard, when it encountered a line of thunderstorms. Vicious winds soon tore the helpless dirigible into three sections. Two immediately fell to Earth. One hit violently, killing those inside. But the other floated gently to the ground and landed in a grove of trees, which cushioned the fall. Most of the crewmen in this part of the ship survived.

The third section of the airship, though, was swept straight up in a powerful air current. Within seconds it had risen to an altitude of almost ten thousand feet—still low enough for the men to breathe, but far above a zeppelin's usual altitude. Among the seven men inside was Lieutenant Commander Charles Rosendahl. Although the situation seemed hopeless, Rosendahl refused to give up. He saw that the remaining half of the airship was functioning much like a balloon, with several gas cells still in place; moreover, he had water and gasoline to use as ballast. As calmly as he could, Rosendahl organized his remaining men to help him bring the craft in for a landing.

As the *Shenandoah* careened around the sky, the men set to work. They opened a valve to let some of the helium escape, which brought the zeppelin gradually toward the ground. Just before landing, though, a sudden gust of wind caught the craft. Rosendahl quickly ordered some of the ballast dropped, allowing the airship to float up once again before the wind could dash it to pieces. One crewman fell out during this maneuver; though badly hurt, he survived.

The next attempt was luckier. "Gradually we settled," Rosendahl recalled afterward, as quoted in Rick Archbold and Ken Marschall's book, *Hindenburg: An Illustrated History*, "and made contact with good old terra firma [Earth] so gently that not even an egg would have cracked." In all, an astonishing twenty-nine of the forty-three men on board survived the wreck of the *Shenandoah*.

entertainments included films and informal concerts. And stewards, cooks, and other service personnel aboard the airship helped make the passengers' journey as smooth and as pleasurable as possible.

First Flights

The *Hindenburg* quickly became one of the most famous aircrafts anywhere on Earth. Put into service in early 1936, the zeppelin began by making a round-trip flight between Rio de Janeiro, Brazil, and its home base in southern Germany. Later that spring, it made its first trip across the North Atlantic. The journey from Germany to the zeppelin's landing site at a naval base in Lakehurst, New Jersey, took just sixty hours. In both financial and technological terms, the trip was a brilliant success.

By the end of 1936, the airship had made a total of sixteen flights across the Atlantic. Once an enormous barrier to intercontinental travel, the ocean no longer seemed an obstacle. Wealthy business travelers and curiosity seekers alike hurried to book their seats. Despite the staggering cost of a one-way ticket— four hundred dollars, approximately the price of a new car in those days—the airship was cheaper than passage on a luxury liner. In most cases, it was faster, too, and the view was even more splendid.

But to ride the *Hindenburg* was to do more than simply cross the Atlantic. Boarding the airship provided a glimpse into a grand technological future, a future in which regularly scheduled zeppelin flights across the Atlantic Ocean would be commonplace. Before cold weather put a temporary stop to

The Hindenburg *flies over New York City. The German airship made its first trip across the Atlantic in the spring of 1936.*

flights in late 1936, more than twenty-six hundred passengers had ridden in luxury between Germany and the Americas aboard the *Hindenburg*.

The future looked bright for zeppelins in general, and the *Hindenburg* in particular. As Harold G. Dick wrote, the manufacturers of the *Hindenburg* "were now enjoying a dazzling success in maintaining an accident-free service, with enormous amounts of favorable publicity, not only in the newspapers of the world but in the excited testimony of delighted passengers."[39] And when 1937 began with another successful round-trip to Brazil, the confidence level of manufacturers, crew, and passengers rose even higher. Zeppelins, it seemed, would be a fixture of international air travel for many years to come.

To New Jersey

On the evening of May 3, 1937, the *Hindenburg* lifted off for New Jersey—its first of eighteen scheduled round-trip flights across the North Atlantic that year. Although passenger capacity had been expanded during the winter to seventy-two, this flight was less than fully booked. Indeed, just thirty-six people had purchased tickets to fly to New Jersey. No one was much dismayed, however: it was early in the season, and the return flight was already sold out. Sixty-one crew members were also aboard, bringing the total on that flight of the *Hindenburg* to ninety-seven.

The crossing over the Atlantic was more difficult than usual. The airship fought against strong westerly winds, delaying it considerably. When the *Hindenburg* finally approached Lakehurst, strong winds and thunderstorms were lashing the area. Mindful of zeppelins' difficulties with bad weather, captain Max Pruss decided to steer clear of the disturbances. Notifying the ground crew of his intentions, he began instead to make a lazy circle through the clearer skies elsewhere in central New Jersey.

Just before 7:00 that evening, over twelve hours after the original landing time, the wind died down and the storm clouds parted. "Conditions definitely improving," the head of the Lakehurst ground crew informed Pruss by radio. "Recommend earliest possible landing."[40] Pruss quickly steered the airship back toward the landing site. At the same time, members of the ground crew hurried onto the landing field. As the zeppelin descended, it would lower lines down to the waiting men. The ground crew would attach the lines to the mooring mast and other fixed points on the ground, helping the craft come in smoothly and gently.

The members of the ground crew were not the only people present for the landing. The American public had not yet become jaded by the transatlantic flights of the previous year. Despite the questionable weather and the rescheduled landing time, a crowd of several hundred onlookers had showed up to watch the airship arrive. The interest extended well beyond Lakehurst, too. Several reporters were on the scene, among them radio broadcaster Herb Morrison of the Chicago station WLS.

To the delight of the crowd, the *Hindenburg* appeared on the horizon shortly after 7 P.M. The zeppelin circled slowly around the landing field, gradually losing altitude as Pruss deftly brought it toward the mooring mast. Crew members aboard the airship dropped the landing lines, and those on the ground seized them as they came down. Morrison began painting a verbal portrait of the experience to his audience over the airwaves. "Here it comes, ladies and gentlemen," he announced, "and what a sight it is, a thrilling one, a marvelous sight."[41]

Unless things went suddenly and dramatically wrong, the great airship would soon be safely landed. And given the Germans' safety record and the accident-free history of the *Hindenburg* itself, neither the passengers, the crew, nor the onlookers had any reason to expect any problems. But as the massive zeppelin began its final approach to the mooring mast, disaster struck.

"Oh, the Humanity!"

The first indication of a possible problem occurred just after 7:20 P.M., when the airship had descended to about one hundred feet above the ground. Crewman Helmut Lau may have heard it first from his perch near the rear control room: a small but unexpected whooshing noise. Later, Lau would describe the sound as similar to the lighting of a gas burner on a stove.

To Lau, the noise seemed to come from somewhere above his head, either on the skin of the zeppelin or in one of the airship's many gas cells. Although he was hard at work trying to untangle a cable, Lau found his attention drawn toward the top of the zeppelin. Other crew members who heard the muffled noise turned to look too. What they saw appalled them.

The mighty zeppelin was burning. Blue and orange flames already covered a small patch of the airship's skin near one of the rear gas cells. Smoke rose swiftly into the evening sky. To this day, the cause of the blaze remains a mystery, and certainly Lau and his fellow crewmen had no idea what had happened. All they knew was that the highly flammable hydrogen gas had caught fire.

The men watched, horrified, as the fire picked up speed and height. A massive fireball began to race along the side of the *Hindenburg*. Seconds later there was another explosion as more hydrogen ignited. Louder and a good deal more powerful than the first, this new explosion blew off the top of the rear portion of the airship. Charred fabric and melted pieces of metal flew through the air.

By this time, the seriousness of the situation was also evident to everyone near the landing field. An American naval official later described the initial spread of the fire as similar to "a mushroom shaped flower bursting speedily into bloom."[42] Other observers were more direct in their choice of words. "It

55

Engulfed in flames, the tail end of the Hindenburg *crashes to the ground.*

is burning, bursting into flames," Herb Morrison told his radio audience. "This is one of the worst catastrophes in the world! . . . Oh, the humanity and all the passengers!"[43]

The leading edge of the fire quickly roared forward. The great airship lurched in the air. Then the rear half of the *Hindenburg*, or what remained of it, dropped slowly toward the ground. It hit with a resounding smash, followed moments later by the now-blazing nose of the zeppelin. Clouds of smoke billowed from the fiery wreck. In less than a minute, a hulk of charred

and twisted metal lay on the ground about seven hundred feet from the mooring mast. It was all that was left of the *Hindenburg*.

Escape

The suddenness of the disaster, the speed at which the fireball traveled, and the fact that the zeppelin was still in the air when the fire broke out—all seemed to make escape unlikely, if not impossible. Indeed, many of the passengers and crew on board the *Hindenburg* that evening were killed either by the fire or by the impact of the crash. In all, thirty-five people on board the *Hindenburg* that evening died either on the scene or in a hospital later on.

But the death toll, in comparison to what it might have been, was startlingly low. Sixty-two people out of the ninety-seven who had originally boarded the zeppelin three days earlier managed to escape the *Hindenburg* before the flames and the crash could kill them. Some were badly burned or required long hospitalizations; a few never made full recoveries from their injuries. But many escaped from the wreck with hardly a scratch.

There were several reasons for the high survival rate. One involved the *Hindenburg*'s rather low altitude. The zeppelin was only about a hundred feet above ground level when the fire began, close enough for people to consider an escape as the airship descended. The low altitude also brought the dirigible down to the ground before it was completely consumed by the flames, thus allowing some passengers and crew members to escape even after the *Hindenburg* had struck the ground.

That the *Hindenburg* was an airship helped too. In contrast to an airplane, which might have hit the ground with far greater force, the zeppelin was built to float gracefully toward the earth. Indeed, the ship fell relatively slowly. A film taken at the scene indicated that the *Hindenburg* took thirty-four seconds to drop the hundred feet. The collision with the ground was certainly jarring, but it was entirely possible for passengers and crew members to survive the impact.

Despite the enormous fire and the crash, sixty-two people escaped the Hindenburg *disaster. Some jumped to safety from the airship's windows.*

Finally, the people on the *Hindenburg* benefited from one important feature of zeppelin construction: the windows in the passenger section, like those in some of the control areas, were designed to be opened. They offered an immediate, if dangerous, option for fleeing the ship. There was no need for passengers or crew members to take the time to smash one of the windows before crawling outside, as would have been the case on most larger airplanes of the time. Along with the low altitude and the slow descent, the windows offered hope to those passengers and crew members who were looking for a way off the flaming ship.

Through the Windows

The actual escape routes used by those aboard the *Hindenburg* varied considerably. Some flung themselves through the windows as quickly as they could manage. Among these survivors was Joseph Späh, a German comedian who lived in New York. Späh slipped through a window in the dining room as soon as he heard the second explosion. The dirigible was still too far aloft to make a safe jump, so he hung tightly to the outside of the ship as it dropped.

When Späh estimated that he was about forty feet above the ground, he let go. The drop was long, but Späh was lithe and flexible. Timing his landing perfectly, he hit the ground, rolled over, and got quickly to his feet. "Whew, am I lucky," Späh later commented to a man who had filmed his precipitous drop. "Not a scratch!"[44]

Others, more cautious and less athletic, did not climb through the windows until the *Hindenburg* was lower still. The zeppelin's chief steward delayed his jump until the airship was less than twenty feet off the ground. Gertrud and Leonhard Adelt planned to squeeze through the promenade windows once the ship actually struck the ground, but changed their minds when furniture began to slide onto them. "The tables and chairs of the reading room crashed about," Leonhard recalled later, "and jammed [against] us like a barricade."[45] Afraid they would be unable to move if they waited, the Adelts jumped; later, they estimated their height from the ground at twelve to fifteen feet.

Crew member Herbert Dowe lingered even longer, though not by choice. Caught inside the dirigible's windowless radio room when the fire broke out, Dowe had to make his way into the control area before he could dive out of the zeppelin. Dowe jumped at what may have been the last possible moment. He had delayed so long that he barely missed being crushed by the burning framework of the *Hindenburg* as he dashed frantically away from the ship.

Not all who dropped from the falling airship escaped through windows, however. Among the most dramatic escapes from the *Hindenburg* was that of fourteen-year-old Werner Franz, who served as a cabin boy aboard the dirigible. Franz found a hatchway in the bottom of the ship, climbed through it, and jumped. Unfortunately, like Herbert Dowe, Franz quickly realized that the

Many people waited until the Hindenburg *hit the ground to escape the inferno.*

burning airship was about to fall on top of him. Worse, by descending through a hatch in the middle of the airship, Franz had left himself no clear path to safety.

Franz began to cough violently as the smoke and flames rose around him. In all likelihood he would have died—except that a water tank over his head suddenly broke open. The water poured down onto his head, clearing his lungs and putting out the fire where he stood. Given a second chance, Franz saw a potential escape route. Dodging the flames, he sprinted to safety—wet but unhurt.

On the Ground

Many of those who escaped, though, did not make a move for freedom until the airship struck the ground. Some of them would gladly have jumped, but they could not find an open window. But most made the choice to stay where they were. They preferred to take their chances with the flames rather than risk a drop of twenty feet or more from the sinking airship. Helmut Lau, the crewman who had originally spotted the fire, was one of several who waited for the impact, then opened a hatch and scurried to safety.

Others did not have such an easy time leaving the burning airship, however. Crew member Richard Kollmer was forced to tear a hole through the outer cover of the zeppelin's skin before he could make his way to safety. Three other crewmen followed him through the gap in the canvas. "I could have won an Olympic gold medal,"[46] Kollmer remarked years afterward, recalling how quickly he darted away from the *Hindenburg.*

In some cases, survivors helped each other escape from the burning wreckage. Crew member Fritz Deeg, for instance, climbed out a window and then turned to assist needy passengers. A mother with two young boys quickly passed her sons to him through an open window. Aware that the airship would soon be consumed in flames, Deeg lost no time getting the boys to safety. He actually threw the first one out of the reach of the fire before hurrying off with the second in his arms. The children's mother survived as well.

Margaret Mather had a similar experience. She had been on the promenade when she first became aware of the fire. The screams of the passengers and the rolling red flames reminded her, she said afterward, of "a scene from a medieval picture of hell."[47] When others around her began to jump, she kept her position. Flames landed on her clothing and her hair, but

The Hindenburg *continued to burn to a bare skeleton of metal even as survivors fled the wreckage.*

The Cause of the Disaster

The cause of the *Hindenburg* fire has never been determined. Those assigned to investigate the crash quickly ruled out many possible causes, but they had little luck determining what had actually happened. As American zeppelin expert Harold G. Dick wrote about a month after the crash, quoted in his book *The Golden Age of the Great Passenger Airships*, "It is becoming increasingly difficult to even advance a theory as to what may have ignited the hydrogen."

The lack of clear evidence, however, has not dissuaded experts and interested observers alike from proposing theories. Many have concluded that the fire was simply a dreadful accident. Investigative panels in both the United States and in Germany eventually attributed the disaster to a sudden buildup in static electricity aboard the aircraft, possibly from nearby thunderstorms. In this theory, the hydrogen ignited when an unusually strong electric charge passed through it. However, both panels indicated that this was only the most likely explanation; neither found the evidence compelling.

Some have suggested that a small tear in the zeppelin's skin could have caused hydrogen to leak suddenly from the cells; the right combination of hydrogen and air could have caused a reaction resulting in fire. Dick was among those who subscribed to this explanation. Others point to a possible stuck valve, a problem with venting the hydrogen cells, or an electrical discharge known as Saint Elmo's fire.

Still others have argued that the disaster was no accident. Many observers, including captain Max Pruss, have said that the fire was a deliberate act of sabotage—most likely caused by a bomb planted among the cells by a German anti-Nazi activist. Certainly the explosion of the *Hindenburg* was a major embarrassment to Hitler's government. Furthermore, a Milwaukee woman had written authorities before the flight, warning them of a potential plot to destroy the airship. However, a theory of sabotage is guesswork at best: no good evidence explains who was responsible for the blast, how the bomb was planted without anyone noticing, or how the detonation was accomplished. What actually caused the blast will likely never be known.

Mather did her best to beat them out with her hands.

Mather was focused so intently on the approaching flames that she did not notice when the airship landed. She might have burned to death where she was, except that several men suddenly saw her on their way out of the aircraft. "Come out, lady!" they called. Startled, Mather stood and was about to follow, when she realized she no longer had her purse. When she began to look for it, one of the men yelled again, "Aren't you coming?"[48] His words returned Mather to reality. Abandoning her search, she hurried out of the burning remains of the airship.

The Escape of Josef Leibrecht

Perhaps the most harrowing escape that evening belonged to the *Hindenburg*'s electrician, Josef Leibrecht. When the fire broke out, Leibrecht was one of twelve crewmen stationed on an interior stairway in the zeppelin's nose. From their position, there was no easy access to the outside. Nor would access necessarily have helped. As the rear of the ship dipped lower, the nose had actually risen. The distance to the ground was thus too great to survive a drop.

Leibrecht and the others resolved to hang on to the stairway. Their hope was to stay where they were and escape once the craft had hit the ground. Unfortunately, the fire was sweeping rapidly in their direction. The dirigible now acted as a funnel, channeling fire and smoke up to the nose. Intense heat seared the men's hands and faces; thick smoke filled their mouths and lungs. In the end, nine of the men could not hang on; they fell into the flames below.

But Leibrecht and two other men did not lose their grip. Later, Leibrecht told a reporter that he had held firm despite the intense heat and lack of oxygen in the last seconds of the descent. When the nose of the airship finally landed, the three men had the presence of mind to release their grips on the hot metal rim of the staircase. Then they dashed through the inferno to safety.

Leibrecht was badly injured in the disaster. His hands and face were burned, his left hand permanently twisted; his body would forever carry scars from the experience. Other survivors would need urgent medical treatment too: Margaret Mather for damaged hands; Leonhard Adelt for serious burns on his scalp. Even Joseph Späh, the acrobatic comedian, developed debilitating leg problems stemming from his forty-foot fall. And nearly all who had escaped would relive the nightmare of that evening again and again.

Still, they had survived. Whether dropping from the windows of the doomed aircraft or climbing through the wreckage once the *Hindenburg* had hit the ground, they had escaped death. They had successfully fled from one of the most famous disasters of their time.

4

Three Mile Island

FOR MOST PEOPLE affected by a man-made disaster, the immediate issue they face is not when or whether to escape, but how. But some types of man-made disasters are different. Sometimes, it is unclear exactly how much danger an accident presents to those in the immediate area. There may be debate about levels of risk; or the potential threat may be more to people's overall health than to their lives. In both circumstances, it can be unclear if escape is a necessity.

A good example of this kind of situation took place in the spring of 1979. That March, a potentially deadly accident took place at the Three Mile Island nuclear reactor in central Pennsylvania. The extent of the danger to people resulting from the accident was widely debated. But in the days after the accident, about 144,000 area residents chose to flee the area—far more than have fled from almost any other catastrophe in American history.

Nuclear Reactors

The problem of producing cheap, reliable, and clean energy has concerned humans since the beginning of recorded history. Sources of energy such as oil, coal, and natural gas, widely used today, all present major drawbacks. Burning them creates pollution; they are inefficient; and most are not renewable. More recently, scientists and engineers have tried obtaining power by harnessing such natural sources as the sun, the wind, and the internal heat of the earth. But for the most part,

63

An atomic bomb test shows the tremendous power of nuclear energy. Scientists began experimenting with nuclear energy during World War II.

wind, they proposed looking instead to the structure of an atom, one of the basic building blocks of all matter. Through various experiments, scientists had discovered how to split the nucleus, or the center of an atom, in half. Moreover, they knew that such a split, known as nuclear fission, would set off a powerful reaction that produced heat and energy.

The first use of this new technology was during World War II, when the United States built several atomic bombs—so named because their destructive force came from splitting the atom—and dropped two of them on Japanese cities. But early on, scientists recognized that nuclear reactions might have peaceful purposes too. In particular, they saw that nuclear fission might provide cheap, efficient energy. The power produced by the split atoms, after all,

these sources have also proved less than ideal.

Around the time of World War II, though, some scientists began searching in a different direction for answers. Rather than harnessing the power of large natural forces such as the sun or the

could be used to make electricity just as easily as making bombs.

Indeed, nuclear energy seemed to hold great promise. Unlike traditional energy plants, which burned oil, coal, or natural gas, the process of splitting the atom sent no plumes of black smoke into the sky. Nuclear energy also promised low costs and impressive efficiency: one ton of uranium, a material often used to generate nuclear power, could produce about as much energy as a million tons of coal. And best of all, atoms, unlike fossil fuels, were inexhaustible.

There were drawbacks, however, to building nuclear reactors—the term most often used for nuclear power plants. The two atomic bombs dropped on Japan had showed the world the destructiveness of uncontained nuclear fission. For reactors, the concern was not so much an explosion as what is called a meltdown. A meltdown is when the material in the reactor's core heats up from the normal operating temperature of 550°F to nearly ten times that high. Among the dramatic consequences of a meltdown would be the release of massive amounts of radiation, energy produced by the reactor's uranium. In large enough doses, radiation causes genetic damage, cancer, and death.

Still, as far as most observers were concerned, the nuclear industry took safety issues seriously. Certainly, the design of reactors minimized the possibility of radiation leaks and other accidents. Steel walls up to a foot thick surrounded the core of the reactor, where the nuclear fission actually takes place. Operating regulations required that the pressure and temperature inside the core be constantly monitored. And reactors were constructed with plenty of fail-safes—automatic systems designed to turn off malfunctioning equipment, release excess pressure, and provide backup alternatives to ensure the smooth running of the plant.

Three Mile Island

The first atomic power plant in the United States was completed in 1957. By early 1979, seventy-two nuclear power plants were in operation around the United States, and an almost equal number were under construction or in the planning stages. To be sure, nuclear power did not prove quite as cheap as its supporters had expected, and questions about safety persisted. Still, the new reactors helped ensure a steady and growing supply of electricity. And in the first two decades of use, there had been no serious nuclear accidents anywhere in America. Nuclear power seemed here to stay in the United States.

But safety concerns loomed larger in the nuclear industry than many observers believed. The 1970s were years of high inflation and soaring construction costs. Few reactors built during this period stayed within their construction budget. As a result, many power companies looked frantically for ways to recoup their investments. One good example of this trend was a reactor constructed at Three Mile Island, a piece of land in Pennsylvania's Susquehanna River, about ten miles south of Harrisburg.

Built to join an already-existing reactor on the same site, this new model was generally known as TMI (for Three Mile Island) Unit 2, or simply Unit 2. Although Unit 2 had been in the planning stages as early as 1967, the facility did not actually go into service until late 1978. By this time, spiraling costs had quintupled the reactor's expected $130 million price tag. Eager to make money, Metropolitan Edison—the energy company that ran Unit 2—outfitted its new plant with equipment and systems that sometimes compromised safety in the pursuit of lower costs and greater efficiency.

The unexpected costs and delays also pushed Metropolitan Edison to put the plant into service before it was ready. Soon after its opening, the plant had to be shut down for two weeks when it developed problems with the cooling system. Over the next three months, a variety of other issues forced shorter shutdowns as well. Some technicians at the facility became disgusted with the constant troubles. "It just was always a disaster," remarked one worker. "The equipment never ran right."[49]

The energy company that owned Pennsylvania's Three Mile Island reactor (pictured) compromised safety at the site to save money.

A handful of people in central Pennsylvania paid attention to the utility's struggles, mishaps, and emphasis on cost cutting. Shortly before the reactor opened, one local antinuclear group published an article that discussed the possibility of a meltdown in the plant. The story argued that thousands of people in the region could die if there were a disaster—and suggested that a nuclear catastrophe might be much more likely than most Pennsylvanians suspected.

Still, few local residents read the article. And not all who did accepted the story's contentions. For the first three months of Unit 2's operation, very few people in the area seriously believed themselves threatened by the new reactor at Three Mile Island. But that mindset would change abruptly at the end of March 1979.

The Crisis Begins

Early in the morning of March 28, technicians at Unit 2 noticed a problem in the system that cooled the reactor's nuclear core. Two pumps designed to circulate water within the core had suddenly stopped working. The operators on duty were not immediately concerned, however. They knew that the reactor had plenty of fail-safes. Other pumps automatically turned on to take over the work of the two that had failed. A relief valve opened to release excess pressure within the core. And the atomic reaction automatically stopped. The crisis seemed to be over.

But alarm bells and warning lights began to go off all over the factory. The trouble was only beginning. Once the pressure inside the core had become normal again, the relief valve was supposed to close. Instead, it stuck open and began to drain cooling water from the system. And although backup pumps automatically went into operation, the liquid draining from the core was not in fact being replaced. Two weeks earlier, plant officials had closed two important valves for maintenance reasons—and then had forgotten to open them again. These closed valves prevented water from reaching the auxiliary pumps, making them useless in pulling fresh water to the rapidly warming core.

By now, the situation was dangerous. With cooling water disappearing from the core, temperatures inside the reactor rose dramatically—as much as 40°F every minute. Unfortunately, the people in the plant had no clear idea of what was going on. An alert designed to report the status of the relief valve was not operating properly; thus, technicians assumed that the valve had shut itself off as scheduled. And despite their zeal to find and fix the problem, no one thought to check the two valves that were supposed to provide more water to the pumps.

Quickly, the operators made their best guess as to what was going on. Their decision, while well intentioned, could not have been more wrong. The core, they decided, was not suffering from too little water, but from too much. Knowing that excess coolant was extremely dangerous in itself, they did the only thing they could: they shut off the last fail-safe, a backup supply of coolant poised to automatically replenish the dwindling water in the core. "The operators thought they were saving the plant by cutting off the emergency water supply," sums up one commentator. "In fact, they had just sealed its fate."[50]

Over the next few hours, the cooling liquid continued to drain away, while the heat inside the reactor's core swelled. By dawn, the temperature was over 2,000°F throughout the entire core, and well above 4,000°F in parts of it. Fortunately, technicians and company officials figured out what was happening before the reactor reached the meltdown temperature of 5,000°F. They quickly took steps to contain the damage and reduce the heat.

But the situation was still far from stable. No one could immediately evaluate what damage had been done to the core. No one could be sure that a meltdown was no longer a possibility. And measurements in and out of the plant made it clear that unacceptable amounts of radiation had been released during the accident. More radiation might well be released in the coming days, too, as engineers struggled to bring the plant back under control.

To Stay or to Leave?

Unlike most other environmental pollutants, radiation is largely undetectable under normal conditions. No clouds of smoke accompany it as it spreads throughout an area; no strong odor alerts those in its path. And while radiation can do horrific damage, the effects are generally not immediate. Where poisonous vapors might make breathing difficult or cause instant skin lesions, radiation typically does not. "It can zap you in your motel room while you're watching [former TV personality] Johnny Carson," wrote a reporter at the time, "and you might not know it for years."[51]

A few people in the area did report certain signs that something was wrong. Those nearest the plant noted a metallic taste in their mouths when they got up. Others heard a roaring sound that may have been related to the escape of the radiation through vents in the reactor. And a handful saw a fine white powder that may have been the result of radioactive particles settling to the ground. But they did not necessarily know what they were experiencing. "Look at the snow on Daddy's pickup,"[52] remarked area resident Ruth Hoover to her children early on the morning of the accident.

For the most part, the people of central Pennsylvania had to rely on plant officials, nuclear scientists, and government authorities to find out what had happened and to determine the level of risk to themselves and to their families. But accurate, reliable information was hard to find, especially during the first two days of the crisis. That was partly because experts legitimately did not know all the answers. Unfortunately, it was also because company officials were not honest

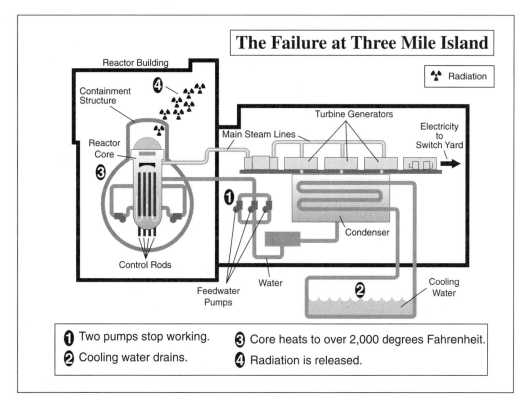

The Failure at Three Mile Island

Reactor Building

Containment Structure

Reactor Core

Control Rods

Main Steam Lines

Turbine Generators

Electricity to Switch Yard

Condenser

Feedwater Pumps

Water

Cooling Water

Radiation

❶ Two pumps stop working.
❷ Cooling water drains.
❸ Core heats to over 2,000 degrees Fahrenheit.
❹ Radiation is released.

about the impact of the disaster. "The radiation releases from the plant," asserted company spokesman Jack Herbein, "are less than that of a dental X ray."[53] The releases, however, were harmful.

Given this contradictory information, some area residents made the decision to carry on with their lives as well as they could. A few accepted the assurances of Metropolitan Edison executives that the damage had been slight and that the problem was under control. "If it was bad, why would the president of the United States come [to the area]?"[54] wondered George Stauffer, pointing out that Jimmy Carter had come to investigate the Three Mile Island facility. And a longtime local

farmer told a reporter, "This doesn't bother me at all."[55]

At the other extreme were some who left the area as quickly as possible. Those living within sight of Three Mile Island were among the first to go. Aware that they were directly in the path of any radiation releases, many of them headed out of town the day of the accident. The next morning, the nearest elementary school to the plant had just one-fifth of its usual attendance. Many pregnant women also left the area right away, as did families with small children. It was widely known that the developing bodies of fetuses and young children made them especially vulnerable to radiation poisoning. To families in this situation, the

Although Three Mile Island never proved as dangerous as the 1986 explosion that destroyed the Chernobyl plant in Ukraine, many Harrisburg residents chose to be safe and evacuate the area.

risks of staying put were simply too great.

Most who lived in the Harrisburg area, however, chose to take a middle ground. Though unconvinced by the utility's assurances, they decided to wait and see. Some noted that there were no calls for immediate evacuation of the area. Trusting in public officials to keep them safe, these people decided to remain where they were as long as they were not instructed to leave.

But as rumors flew around the area, many Pennsylvanians became more

and more uneasy about this choice. And on the morning of Friday, March 30, when Unit 2 accidentally released more radiation into the skies, some of these people decided that staying where they were no longer represented an acceptable risk. Their decision was made easier by reports that a massive hydrogen bubble had been found inside the core of the reactor; this bubble, scientists said, had a significant chance of exploding.

Government leaders, however, did not formally order an evacuation, even then. They only issued a recommendation that small children and pregnant women who lived within five miles of the plant should go elsewhere. But they did close schools, and one radio station reported that a general evacuation order might be on the way. Shaken and worried, thousands of people in the Harrisburg area now decided to take matters into their own hands.

Beginning on the morning of March 30, and continuing for several days afterward, a steady stream of Pennsylvanians loaded up their cars and headed out of town, leaving their homes behind. None knew when they would return, and some had no idea

The Question of Evacuation

In the hours and days following the Three Mile Island disaster, scientists and politicians argued bitterly over several subjects. Among the most contentious of these debates involved the question of evacuation. Part of the debate revolved around the question of whether an evacuation should be ordered—or even recommended. Given the reality of the radiation release and the possibility of more to come, some officials recommended relocation until central Pennsylvania could be declared safe. "[The situation] is on the threshold of turning bad," argued nuclear scientist Roger Mattson, quoted in Daniel F. Ford's book *Three Mile Island: Thirty Minutes to Meltdown.* "I don't have a reason for not moving people [out of the area]."

But others disagreed. Some were unconvinced—or unaware—of the danger. "We don't see any reason for emergency procedures," said utility spokesman Jack Herbein, quoted in Mark Stephens's book *Three Mile Island.* Others asserted that a full-scale evacuation could not be accomplished quickly or easily. The Harrisburg police department, for instance, anticipated that a full evacuation of their city would take at least twenty hours.

And if an evacuation were to be ordered, there was no consensus on which people should be ordered to leave. One scientist recommended that everyone who lived five miles from the plant should be moved out. Another argued that ten miles would be a safer and more reasonable limit. Other officials suggested that plans should be drawn up for a more comprehensive evacuation plan that would encompass all the area within a twenty-mile radius of the damaged reactor.

The eventual decision—to recommend evacuation for pregnant women and small children within a five-mile radius of the plant—was controversial too. Several scientists and emergency personnel felt that the recommendation was entirely too weak. Indeed, the head of the Harrisburg civil defense authority was so angry with the decision that he very nearly declared an evacuation on his own. In the end, the state's lieutenant governor convinced him not to. But the incident demonstrates how raw and tense the situation had become.

where they were going, but all preferred uncertainty to the possibility of a meltdown or further radiation poisoning. By the end of the exodus, an estimated 144,000 people had escaped from the disaster at Three Mile Island.

Family members evacuate their home near the Three Mile Island reactor. Some people left in an orderly fashion, but many others fled in panic.

Escape

While a few area residents left their homes calmly and quietly, that was not true of the majority of the people who fled. Once the radiation leak had been discovered, chaos ensued. Some feared it was already too late. Others wondered whether they were overreacting, even as they began to pack. A few worried about both at once. "I was almost traumatized by the fact that I didn't know . . . if it was all over to begin with," remembered Matt Magda of Harrisburg, "or if I had a chance and should leave now."[56]

The leak was announced shortly after the workday had begun, so families were scattered among schools, stores, and workplaces. As terrified residents heard the news, they tried to get in touch with spouses, children, and friends. But local telephone systems proved unable to handle the volume of calls; getting a dial tone was almost impossible in much of the area. Unable to reach their loved ones, many people began to panic. Assuming the worst, many residents hopped into their cars and went to find friends and relatives. Vehicles soon clogged the local roads. "There were cars whipping around corners," recalled Matt Magda, who drove to his sister-in-law's high school to pick her up shortly after the announcement was made. "It was a madhouse."[57]

As drivers picked up their families and prepared to leave, the panic level steadily grew. Residents had to make quick decisions about what they should or should not take with them. The answers depended in part on an individual's perception of the risk and the length of time he or she expected to be away. The answers were not obvious, but the stakes were huge. "What should I do with my dog?"[58] a frantic caller plaintively asked a radio announcer.

Most people chose to fill their cars with as much as their vehicles could carry. "I saw people outside their houses with all the car doors open," recalled Suzanne Magda, Matt's wife, "just pitching food and clothing and household goods, just throwing them into their cars."[59] But in towns throughout the area, some residents simply drove off as soon as they heard about the release of radiation. "We left so quickly on Friday that we basically took [only] ourselves,"[60] said area resident Marsha McHenry. In their zeal to

As children evacuate, a civil defense worker tests radiation levels at an elementary school near Three Mile Island.

escape, many of these people did not even lock their doors or turn off their radios. At that moment, ensuring their own safety was far more significant than securing their property.

Metropolitan Edison

Many commentators, during and after the incident at Three Mile Island, have assigned Metropolitan Edison the largest share of blame for the disaster. Questions arose about the design of the facility almost from the beginning of its existence, with charges that the utility company was compromising safety in an effort to cut costs. The relief valve that accidentally drained the water from the core, for example, was part of an inexpensive system noted for unreliability. Likewise, the training of workers at the nuclear plant seems to have been less than complete.

Moreover, Metropolitan Edison was a good deal less than forthcoming as the disaster unfolded. Supervisors took their time alerting local authorities to the problems; it was three hours before anyone called local emergency services. Even then, they did their best to confuse the issue. On the morning of the disaster, company officials assured Lieutenant Governor William Scranton that everything was under control at the plant, and that there were no risks to anyone's life and health. Relieved, Scranton passed the information on to reporters at a press conference. A few minutes later, though, he learned from other sources that radiation had been released in the accident. This sort of deliberate misinformation, given by those who were in the best position to know the truth, gave the plant and its officials a bad name—and, of course, added to the widespread uncertainty over what had actually taken place.

Expecting the Worst

As the day continued, the mood grew ever more anxious and alarming. Even those residents who were determined to stay found their resolve weakening as they watched their friends and neighbors leaving town. Most people of the area doubted or dismissed as false any positive news about the plant. Virtually no one paid attention when an inspector at the plant announced that "preventive actions were being taken" to take care of the problems, and that evacuation measures were a "total mistake."[61] Nor were most residents reassured when officials announced—correctly, as it developed—that they had overstated the amount of radiation released that morning. Negative reports, in contrast, found a receptive and increasingly frightened audience.

As the day wore on, residents redoubled their efforts to get out of town before it would be too late. In some cases, their actions bordered on the bizarre. A handful of hysterical residents, afraid that they would lose the investment they had made in their homes, offered their properties for sale to anyone who would pay cash. (No sales were reported.) Others, lacking reliable transportation, drove their old vehicles to car lots and bought new models on the spot. "Nobody even wanted to haggle,"[62] remarked a dealer who set a new sales record that day.

To prepare for their escape, terrified residents poured into banks and grocery stores. On Friday morning, the Federal Reserve shipped $7 million to local banks to cover the enormous demand for cash. The extra money was necessary, as some customers withdrew thousands of dollars from their accounts. Supermarkets, in the meantime, ran low on canned goods, milk, and other items. The situation was made worse when many smaller stores simply shut down so their owners and employees could leave town themselves.

But the longest lines were at local gas stations. Worried about running low on fuel, thousands of area drivers stopped to fill up their tanks before they made their escape. Lines snaked around corners and sometimes covered two city blocks. Tempers rose as drivers inched forward. "People [were] desperate . . . ," recalled Suzanne Magda, "being very demanding, screaming, and filling their cars with gas."[63]

A few local residents were prepared for the worst. To them, though, the danger lay not so much with the nuclear reactor as with other drivers seeking refuge. Marsha McHenry's neighbor urged her to follow him as she left town. He had weapons and a chain saw, he informed her, and he would not hesitate to destroy barriers that blocked his way to safety. "I got my piece in the trunk," another local man told a reporter, referring to his gun. "If the turnpike gets jammed, I'll shoot my way out."[64]

"We Went to Illinois"

The gun was unnecessary, as it turned out; so was McHenry's neighbor's chain saw. In fact, there was probably more cooperation around the area than there was hostility. In many places, residents looked after each other, ensuring that those who did not have cars rode with those who did. Police officers and medical personnel remained on the job. One nursing home evacuated all forty of its patients to a hospital fifteen miles farther from Three Mile Island; the entire procedure took less than two hours.

Moreover, while traffic was heavy at times and the mood tense, there were few altercations reported as people began to leave. And once people were on the highways, the congestion dwindled considerably. Here, the region's geography was helpful. Unlike the people of coastal towns or mountain villages, there were not just one or two ways out of the area. Instead, the residents of the affected zone could travel out of town in almost any direction they chose.

Some of the refugees hurried to emergency shelters set up in nearby counties by civil defense authorities. One of the largest of these was in the town of Hershey, where a sports arena was turned into temporary housing. Most of those who fled, however, preferred to go farther afield. Hershey, less than fifty miles east of Harrisburg, was simply too close to Three Mile Island. Still, some families who had nowhere else to go were pleased to have the option.

The bulk of escaping residents moved in with friends and family members. Again, some chose to stay relatively close to home. But others traveled

Harrisburg residents who decided to evacuate in the wake of the disaster faced long lines at gas stations.

farther. "We evacuated our three children and our pets to Philadelphia Friday evening, to my mother's home,"[65] reported a nurse married to a doctor. Because of their jobs and the potential need for trained medical staff, the couple returned to work the following day, leaving their children behind.

And some thought that even Philadelphia was too close. The Magdas went first to Connecticut, where they stayed with relatives. Then, worried that radiation might penetrate even that far, they moved on to a friend's home in Boston. Others traveled to Florida, the Midwest, or even the West Coast. "We went and left the state and went to Illinois to our aunt and uncle's house,"[66] reported a fifth-grade student.

In many parts of the area, the result of the exodus was clear and dramatic. Entire towns emptied out, especially those nearest the damaged reactor. Middletown was almost deserted. Goldsboro was even worse. On Saturday morning, a reporter visiting Goldsboro found no signs of human activity. The few residents remaining had elected to stay inside. Only silent houses and empty streets met his eye. "It was one of the eeriest feelings I had ever had in my life,"[67] he later wrote.

Even in Harrisburg and other communities more distant from Three Mile Island, the drop in population was noticeable. And the situation became even more obvious on Saturday, March 31, when a report began to circulate through the area that the hydrogen bubble would surely burst in a few hours. The number of cars leaving the area had dwindled somewhat since the panic of Friday. Now, many of those who had stayed rethought their decision. Once again, gas lines lengthened, frantic residents stuffed clothing and canned foods into their cars, and the exodus began anew.

The Aftermath

Saturday's alarm about the explosiveness of the hydrogen bubble was immediately challenged by officials on the scene. The report, they said, was wrong. If an explosion were inevitable, or if the bubble were to cause a meltdown, scientists would certainly have more than a few hours' notice. At first the correction, though accurate, did little to soothe jangled nerves in and around Harrisburg. Families continued to leave the area throughout the weekend and even into Monday morning. Even the Pennsylvania state government drew up evacuation plans.

On Monday morning, government leaders announced a news conference to discuss the situation. Convinced that authorities would order a complete

A nuclear engineer prepares to enter the Three Mile Island reactor core. By closely monitoring the reactor, officials were able to avert a meltdown.

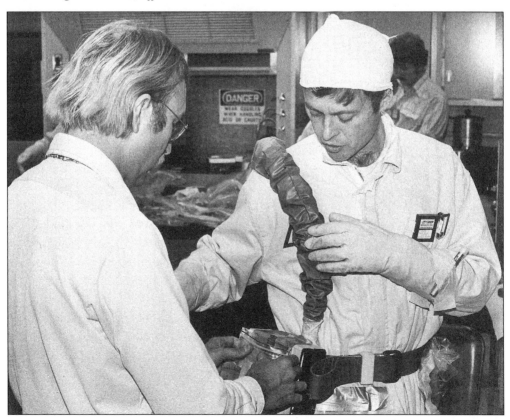

Many who fled the area were concerned with the long-term effects of nuclear radiation. This boy was born with disfigured hands after the Chernobyl meltdown.

the plant, the crisis had been averted. Radiation readings outside the plant had dropped toward normal levels. Slowly, residents began to trickle back to their homes. As the bubble continued to shrink, scientists realized that the bubble was not going to explode; this information reassured many who were still uneasy about whether they should return. By Friday, April 6, most of the people of the area had come home.

Some of those who returned were slightly embarrassed by their flight. Because the disaster had ended without a meltdown, they wondered if they had been hasty. But most were glad that they had left town when they did. The long-term radiation effects of the Three Mile Island disaster are yet to be known. Though the radiation releases were invisible and short-lived, they nonetheless presented a serious danger to the people of the area. Escape, even for a period of three or four days, may have helped thousands of people avoid developing cancers and other health problems. Given what they knew and what they feared might take place, there was every reason for the people of the area to escape the region when they did.

evacuation, many of those who still remained in the area spent the early morning hours packing. "We had everything ready to go,"[68] said area resident Ron Miller. But instead, the conference offered good news. The bubble, officials announced, was shrinking. And the water being pumped into the reactor's core was bringing down the temperature.

By Tuesday, April 3, the situation was clearly improved. While much work still remained to be done inside

5

Escape from the World Trade Center

Until September 11, 2001, the World Trade Center in lower Manhattan stood as one of the most famous architectural symbols of the United States. The two office towers that made up the bulk of the complex each rose 110 stories above the ground, making them among the tallest buildings in the world. The towers dominated the New York City skyline, their images appearing on New York souvenirs from T-shirts to postcards. The complex served as headquarters to some of America's wealthiest trading firms.

But in a few hours on the morning of September 11, the complex was tragically destroyed. The twin towers, proud symbols of American wealth and commerce, became the target of a violent and deadly attack from radical Islamic terrorists. While close to three thousand people lost their lives in the disaster, thousands more managed to escape the destruction of the towers. Their stories are harrowing and dramatic.

Hijackings and Terrorists

The circumstances of the September 11 terrorist attacks are well known today. Early that morning, nineteen terrorists affiliated with the radical Islamic group al-Qaeda commandeered four passenger aircraft flying over the eastern United States. As part of a well-coordinated plan to destroy American lives and property, the men used the airplanes as flying bombs by steering them into American buildings.

The terrorists' plans were not completely successful. Because of a delay in taking off, one of the four flights was hijacked long after the others. Through cell phone calls to family and friends, passengers learned of the hijackers' intentions before the plane reached the building it was supposed to hit. (The exact identity of this building remains unknown.) A group of passengers stormed the cockpit and tried to take control of the plane. A few minutes later, the flight crashed in a Pennsylvania field, killing all aboard. The result was tragic, but the passengers' courage had kept at least one American building, and the people within it, from harm.

The other three airplanes, however, met their targets. One was sent spinning into a wall of the Pentagon, the massive defense complex across the Potomac River from Washington, D.C. Although the airplane missed the most vulnerable spots along the building's perimeter, the impact nevertheless damaged a large section of the complex. One hundred and twenty-five employees and visitors that morning were killed; many more were wounded. And once again, all aboard the airplane—passengers, crew, and hijackers alike—died as well.

"I Knew This Was No Accident"

The deadliest of the flights, though, struck the World Trade Center. The first of the four airplanes to be hijacked was American Airlines Flight 11, scheduled to fly from Massachusetts to California. When the plane was over Albany, New York, though, the terrorists made their move. Taking the crew by surprise, they seized the controls of the plane. Then they flew along the Hudson River toward lower Manhattan.

As the flight approached New York City, the plane descended rapidly. Many observers would later recall how Flight 11's unexpected path captured their attention. "Hey, that plane's flying kind of low,"[69] one man remembered telling a friend as he watched the plane speeding along less than a thousand feet above his head. And Joan Fleischer, who lived just a few blocks from the World Trade Center complex, said afterward that she was certain it was about to crash. The only question, she added, was where.

The clear answer, had Fleischer had the time to think through the situation, was the World Trade Center. The two towers of the center stuck far up into the sky—a few hundred feet above the jet's current altitude. Moreover, they lay almost directly in the line of the hijacked plane's path. As Fleischer watched in horror from the roof of her apartment building, Flight 11 struck the ninety-second floor of the north tower. "Its speed," she said later, "propelled the plane completely inside the building."[70]

Thick smoke billowed out into the morning skies, and fireballs began to appear at the point of impact. Shocked onlookers gathered and stared at the sight. Most believed at first that the crash had been a mistake—a fatal error of a rookie pilot, perhaps, or a mechanical failure with tragic consequences. Still, even then, a few suspected a terrorist attack. "I knew this was no accident," reported firefighter Richard Picciotto afterward. "I knew this in my gut, and I knew this in my heart, and I knew this in my head."[71]

The impact of the airplane against the walls of the north tower instantly killed everyone aboard the aircraft. But the body of the plane continued forward even after the impact, skidding through walls and slicing office partitions in two. Most workers on the ninety-second floor were killed instantly as the airplane came rushing through. Jet fuel quickly ignited. Soon much of the floor was in flames.

Sadly, there would be no escape for anyone on the north tower's ninety-second floor that day. Nor would anyone above that part of the building reach safety. The fire was too strong, too hot, and too sudden. Moreover, the structural damage created by the airplane blocked the tower's stairwells between the ninety-first and ninety-second floors and destroyed the elevator shafts that far up as well. Without an escape route to the base of the tower, the people at and above the airplane's point of impact were doomed.

The south tower of the World Trade Center explodes with the impact of the second plane as the north tower burns on September 11, 2001.

Evacuation Plans

But most of the people in the north tower at that point were safely below the ninety-second floor. Directly after the crash, they had a clear path down to the building's lobby and the safety of the outside. However, many people in this tower had no idea what had just happened. The thick walls of the building muffled the sound and the force of the impact for most people below the ninety-second floor. Other than a handful of workers who happened to be looking out the window as Flight 11 crashed, no one had reason to think that an airplane had hit the building. Some wondered if there had been an explosion several blocks away. And one worker remembered thinking that someone had simply dropped a very large file cabinet.

With no clear sense of the danger, many people felt no urgency to evacuate the building. And even as phone calls and eyewitness accounts began to reveal the truth, not everyone was eager to leave their offices. Given that the fire was limited to the upper floors of the building, most people saw no reason why they were in any danger.

A similar debate began to rage next door in the south tower. Some workers in this building had felt the impact of the crash. "There was smoke, black and gray," remembered Clyde Ebanks. "We

Prevented from evacuating by the searing fire below them, office workers above the north tower's ninety-second floor cry for help.

all huddled around the window and that's when I could feel the heat."[72] Some in the south tower urged immediate evacuation. Most feared that the fire might spread to their own building. A few suspected that they might be the next target. But just like in the north tower, others insisted on staying put.

The truth was, evacuating the buildings would be time-consuming and inconvenient at best. The evacuation route led down dozens of flights of stairs. (Elevator use in emergencies is discouraged for several reasons, among them the possibility that a sudden shutdown of power could leave passengers trapped between floors.) The three stairways leading down the height of the building were navigable, but they were narrow, dark, and—most of all—long. Even for physically fit workers, the trek downstairs would take precious time from the workday ahead. "I don't want to waste the morning,"[73] one man told a colleague who suggested that they leave.

For less able workers, the thought of descending forty, sixty, or eighty floors was much more alarming. Some who walked slowly or with great effort knew they would have terrible difficulty with the stairs. "I'm an asthmatic," recalled one man after the tragedy, "so the thought of going down fifty-five flights was a little overwhelming."[74]

And for those who could not walk at all, evacuation was impossible without help. After a bomb went off in the World Trade Center parking garage in 1993, management had insisted that disabled workers at the tower have access to special evacuation chairs. The workers would sit in these chairs while colleagues or rescue personnel carried them down the steps. But not every disabled worker in the tower had one, and those who did were not sure that they could rely on others to get them safely to the lobby.

Escape Down the Stairs

Still, some people in both towers immediately started down the steps. Among them were a handful of people who had experienced the attack firsthand. In his ninety-first floor north tower office, for instance, George Sleigh actually saw the underbelly of the plane sliding above him. "Everything just crumbled," he said later. "My office collapsed instantaneously."[75] For Sleigh and others in this position, staying put was clearly not an option.

Those who did start to evacuate found that progress was slow, sometimes agonizingly so. Descending fifteen floors on the upper reaches of the south tower took one man ten minutes. And conditions slowed considerably lower down, as many thousands of people from an ever-increasing number of offices funneled into the three stairways. "It was a single-file situation," reported Roy Bell, who ran into heavy traffic at the fortieth floor of the north tower. "People were merging at every landing."[76]

Another issue was smoke and debris. Billowing clouds of smoke began to fill the stairwells, making visibility difficult and breathing a challenge. One group of

Computers and Palm Pilots

The companies that had offices in the towers of the World Trade Center tended to be wealthy, successful, and demanding. Their employees, in turn, were highly educated, highly motivated, and highly skilled. For many of these men and women, their work was their life. In most of these companies, few employees kept ordinary nine-to-five working hours. Instead, they were in their offices early and stayed at their desks till late. Their determination was exemplary. But in some cases, it cost them their lives.

For example, although the first plane hit about fifteen minutes before 9:00 that morning, many workers were already in the towers. Some firms had scheduled meetings that began at 8 A.M. or even earlier; others were employees catching up on back assignments or getting a head start on new projects. From all accounts, few minded the extra hours and the heavy workload. But it was the early arrivals who were disproportionately affected by the disaster. Those coming to work late—or in some cases, on time—never walked into the complex at all.

And even when they knew they had to evacuate, many workers found themselves unable to simply leave their offices and walk down the stairs. Quite a few, even in the areas closest to the points of impact, took the time to make backup disks, download information onto Palm Pilots, and print out essential company data. Some packed up laptop computers; a few even tried to take bulky desktop equipment with them.

Richard Picciotto, who helped spearhead the evacuation in the north tower, was shocked to find one man working long after everyone should have left. Picciotto ordered the man to leave instantly, but the man held up his hand. "Wait a minute, buddy," he said, as quoted in Picciotto's book *Last Man Down*. "I got something important here." The fate of this man is not recorded, and no one knows how many of the dead were killed because they could not quite pull themselves away from the work that defined them. But certainly the unwillingness to leave at once contributed to the death toll in the disaster.

workers from an office on the north tower's eighty-seventh floor formed a human chain to get down the first few flights of steps, each person with a hand on the shoulder of the one in front. Similarly, flying debris from the wreck blocked several stairwells. One group had to switch stairs at the forty-fourth floor.

Although the stairways began to fill with people, most of them were walking calmly. People waited their turns to move ahead, and many stopped to offer each other assistance. "There was no question of whether they were going to bring me,"[77] recalled John Abruzzo of his colleagues, who carried him down sixty-nine floors in an evacuation chair.

Frustrated by the slow pace, a few people toward the top of the south tower went against policy and chose to use an elevator instead. "The thought of walking down seventy-eight floors in my high heels was not exactly something I wanted to do,"[78] recalled Lori Guarnera, who turned to the elevators after descending twenty-five flights of stairs. Guarnera was lucky. The elevator she boarded brought her safely to the lobby—moments before the next tragic impact.

But for others, elevators were a much more serious hazard. Roy Bell, who noted the amount of traffic in the lower stairwells of the north tower, was on an elevator at the seventy-eighth floor when Flight 11 struck. The fire fourteen stories above him immediately began and quickly raged out of control. The blaze was so big that it pulled in extra oxygen from any other available source—including the shaft of Bell's elevator, which now began to function as a massive chimney.

In an instant, a fireball came barreling down the shaft, sucking all the oxygen and knocking most of the people in the area to the ground. Fortunately for Bell, the elevator doors were open at the moment of impact; the car had come to a stop to let people off. Quickly, he bolted through the open door and down the hall to the nearest stairwell. Another passenger, Virginia DiChiria, dived through the flames to follow him.

Bell received second-degree burns in the fire, and DiChiria's injuries were considerably worse; but their quick reactions had saved their lives.

Other people became stuck inside elevators. Just before Flight 11 hit the

Office workers file down a smoky stairwell as they evacuate the World Trade Center.

The south tower of the World Trade Center explodes after being hit by the airplane. As the fireball blew through the building, it trapped several people inside elevators.

north tower, Michael Jacobs had boarded an elevator in the building's lobby. He and his fellow passengers had gone just a few floors when the airplane hit. At first, Jacobs assumed it was only a minor malfunction and that things would soon resolve themselves. "Don't worry," he told the other people inside the car. "Read your paper. I'll drink my coffee."[79]

But as time passed and no one came to their aid, Jacobs grew concerned. Deciding to try to pry open the doors of the elevator instead, he managed to force the doors far enough apart for the

people inside to squeeze through. Much to their surprise, their elevator had fallen all the way back to the first floor. Frightened but unhurt, the group walked into the lobby and out the front door.

Six men elsewhere in the north tower had an even more frightening experience. The plane had evidently cut a cable in the elevator shaft overhead, and the car they were in started to plummet. One of the men quickly pushed the emergency stop button, forcing the car to stop abruptly on the fiftieth floor. The men in this elevator quickly pried open the doors. But they were riding an express elevator that did not stop at every floor. At the fiftieth floor, in fact, there was no opening to the elevator shaft. Only a blank wall met their eyes.

Staying put was not a possibility; the elevator shaft was rapidly filling with smoke. And unlike Jacobs, they did not expect that help would soon be on the way. Luckily, one of the men, window washer Jan Demczur, had an idea. Seeing that the wall in front of them was made of thick plasterboard, not reinforced concrete, Demczur proposed that the men try to cut their way to safety. They had no knives or other sharp objects among them, but Demczur did have his window washing squeegee.

Tirelessly Demczur attacked the wall with the tool's metal edge. Later, when he accidentally dropped it down the shaft, Demczur switched to using a squeegee handle. The work was tedious and frustrating, but after half an hour the men had succeeded in chopping a hole through the plasterboard. Then they knocked out a few tiles in the wall behind. That led them into a bathroom on the fiftieth floor. One by one, the men crawled through the hole they had created. Then they made for the staircases. All six survived.

The Towers Collapse

Just after 9 A.M., about fifteen minutes after Flight 11 collided with the north tower, Flight 175 came flying over lower Manhattan. Like the first, this one was flying dangerously low—and ominously fast. As people on the ground

watched in horror, the second plane crashed into the outer wall of the one undamaged tower.

Those not killed by this crash now knew that the first disaster was not an accident. For all anyone knew, even more jets were on their way. In both buildings, people hurried out of their offices toward the nearest stairwell to join those who were already making their way down the steps.

Their goal was to reach the safety of the lobby below. "Mobs of people were coming out" into the lobby, remembered Mickey Kross, a firefighter who helped with the evacuation. "[Some had] skin hanging off, [their] clothes disheveled."[80] Most, however, were still in reasonable physical condition. Once in the buildings' lobbies, the workers hurried out into the late summer morning.

But the terror was not yet over. The superheated fire on the towers' uppermost floors had begun to melt the supports that held the buildings upright. The two towers were rapidly approaching instability. At about 10:00 that morning, the south tower slowly began to fall. "I watched in horror as the top floors peeled off like a banana," remembered a man standing nearby, "and started coming straight down toward us."[81]

The tower collapsed with a tremendous roar. Debris flew everywhere, and a cloud of black smoke rose from the ruins. "It was the darkest black I've ever been in,"[82] recalled one man in the crowd below. The other tower followed suit shortly thereafter. Across much of the country, people stared, uncomprehending, at their television screens. Where the twin towers of the World Trade Center had stood just a few hours earlier, now there was nothingness.

Trapped in the Ruins

At the moment of disintegration, the south tower, in particular, was still filled with workers streaming down the stairs toward the exits. Only about an hour had elapsed between the time the tower was hit and the time it fell. Although thousands of people were safely evacuated during that period, there had not been enough time to get everyone out.

People in the north tower had a little more time to make their escape, and later reports suggested that nearly all the workers below the ninety-second floor got out safely. However, soon after the first plane struck, rescue workers had poured into both towers to assist survivors and to see if they could contain the damage to the buildings. As people came down the stairs, they met rescue workers climbing up. Over four

The Top Floors of the South Tower

Unlike Flight 11, Flight 175 struck the south tower obliquely rather than head-on. It also was going about 100 mph faster than the first plane's speed. In most respects, the greatest and most immediate structural damage was caused by the second plane; that was one of the reasons the south tower, though second to be hit, was the first to collapse. However, the difference in impact provided some hope for those stuck in the south tower's uppermost floors because rubble from the disaster filled only two of the south tower's three stairwells.

To be sure, most of the people above the point of impact in the south tower died in the disaster. Those who perished did not stumble on the one unblocked stairway. Moreover, some who did discover the stairway made the fateful choice to go up to the roof of the building rather than down to the lobby. They had hopes of being rescued by helicopter, if that became necessary. Unfortunately, the entrance to the roof was locked; nor is it clear that helicopters could have made a difference. In any case, all who tried to use this way out were killed.

Still, a few people on the uppermost floors of the south tower that morning did survive. Some had left their desks immediately after realizing that Flight 11 had struck the other tower. By the time Flight 175 struck their own building, they were safely below the point of impact. And others, who had delayed longer than they should have, were fortunate enough to find the one stairwell undisturbed by the crash. If they moved quickly enough, and some did, they were out of the lobby by the time the tower collapsed. As a result, being above the point of impact in the south tower was not the automatic death sentence it had been in the north tower.

The south tower crashes to the ground about an hour after being struck by the hijacked airplane. The north tower followed soon after.

hundred emergency personnel, most of them firefighters, died that day when the buildings fell onto them.

Yet not everyone caught inside the World Trade Center was killed when the towers fell because the buildings did not smash evenly against the ground. Rather than covering the ground with thick layers of rubble, the buildings fell haphazardly. Concrete blocks and other building materials formed protective air pockets, empty spaces several cubic yards in volume. A small number of people survived the collapse by falling into one of these pockets—and making their way out.

The most dramatic of these stories involved the experience of a group of firefighters in the north tower. They were on the sixth or seventh floor of the building when Mickey Kross, one of the rescuers, felt what he described later as "a sense of tremendous energy, like being on a locomotive track with a train coming at you."[83] It was the sound of the building collapsing on them.

Escape from Outside

The people inside the towers of the World Trade Center were not the only New Yorkers whose lives were in danger on September 11, 2001. Many people were forced to run for their lives as the towers came tumbling down. Though no one knows the exact death toll outside the center that day, some of the onlookers—including a few who had safely descended from their offices in the towers—were killed by flying debris, or were choked as ash and particles rained down upon them.

Even for those who survived, getting out of the area was not easy. Christian Martin, an observer at the scene, began to sprint away from the complex as the south tower collapsed. He was almost too late. A powerful and speedy cloud of dust, ash, and chunks of concrete swept toward him, picked him up, and hurled him about twenty feet forward. Martin hit an object—exactly what it was, he did not know—and landed on the sidewalk. "I could not see anything," Martin reported later, as quoted in Allison Gilbert, ed., *Covering Catastrophe.* "Not even my hand in front of my face."

Trying to keep himself safe, Martin attempted to burrow underneath a parked car. But he was unable to fit. Besides, he kept choking on pieces of ash. Instead, Martin picked himself up and stumbled off into the blackness. As he walked, coughing violently, the smoke gradually began to lift. Soon he found himself outside a building, where two men offered him something to drink.

The drink cleared his throat considerably and eased the intensity of his cough. Martin realized now that he was not as badly injured as he had feared. Finding a phone, he called his wife, and was reunited with her a few hours later. Martin's was one of hundreds of similar stories among the people who watched the towers fall that morning.

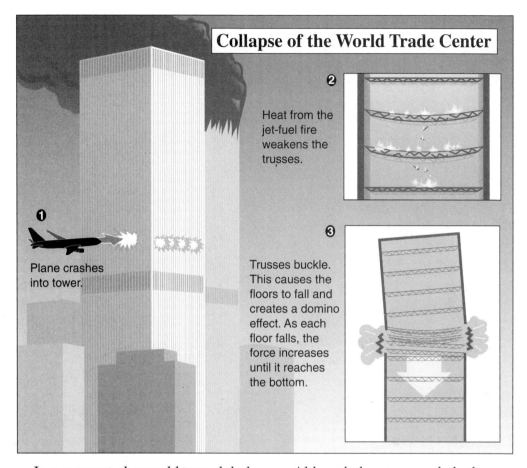

Collapse of the World Trade Center

❶ Plane crashes into tower.

❷ Heat from the jet-fuel fire weakens the trusses.

❸ Trusses buckle. This causes the floors to fall and creates a domino effect. As each floor falls, the force increases until it reaches the bottom.

In a moment, the world turned dark and the floor below the rescuers plummeted. Richard Picciotto remembered afterward not falling so much as sliding down piles of rubble. "I was a big piece of debris," he wrote later, "hurtling through the shell of that stairwell."[84] Some of the rescue workers were injured in the crash. But as they came to a stop, their fall cushioned by the constant bounces off the debris, they realized that most of them were alive. Not only that, they had with them Josephine Harris, a worker who had been having difficulty descending the steps; and she, too, was alive.

Although the area was dark, the rescuers used emergency flashlights to see where they were. They quickly discovered that they were in a sort of cavern surrounded by building materials. At first, the firefighters tried calling for help on their emergency radios. But when they could not make contact, they decided to look for a way out. Those who were most mobile picked their way across the rubble and jimmied a locked door. Unfortunately, their work was in vain. The door only led to another space even more full of debris than the one where they were trapped.

New Yorkers on the street flee a cloud of smoke and debris as the south tower collapses.

Up to the Light

Not only did the door not lead to safety, but they had wasted valuable time and energy. There seemed to be no oth-

er way out. Growing frantic, Picciotto tried again to summon assistance. This time, he managed to make contact with another rescue worker outside the tower. But he learned, to his dismay, that the entire building had collapsed. There were no longer any reference points to help find the group. Worse yet, a mountain of rubble stood between them and the outside.

For an hour or two they stayed put, wondering what to do. But as the smoke around them cleared, they realized that their prison seemed to be getting lighter. After a time it became evident that there was a hole in the debris above them. "Sunlight came right through," Kross told a reporter later on. "A beam of sunlight maybe about six to eight to ten inches—very small and narrow, but it came right into where we were."[85]

The sight gave them hope. Not only did this provide a supply of air and light, but it also offered a possible way out. The distance to the hole was about forty feet—a long way to go, but not out of the question. Moreover, the stairwell down which they had tumbled was still intact in places above their heads. Picciotto, the highest-ranking official in the group, went first. Slowly and carefully, he clambered up toward the empty space as the others watched.

The going was far from smooth. In some places, there were gaps in the stairway where concrete chunks had fallen out. In others, rubble blocked Picciotto's path. But he persevered—and reached the edge of the hole. Seeing that he could do it, the others moved up to join him. Some had an easier time of it than Picciotto. Others had to travel across concrete blocks and

jagged beams. A few helped Josephine Harris across the pile as well.

On the other side of the hole, a massive pile of debris led down to the safety of the street. There was no way that Harris could navigate this stretch, even with help, and so a few of the rescue workers stayed with her. The others, however, decided to try crossing the debris rather than waiting for help to arrive.

Picciotto went first. He picked his way slowly across the rubble, setting up a rope for others to use in their own descent. In places, the ruins still smoldered. In some spots, empty chasms loomed; in others, sharp drops required intense concentration and physical effort. Little by little, Picciotto inched along, blazing a trail for the others to follow.

The climb across the pile of rubble was hazardous and frightening. More than once, some of them wondered if they could go on. But like Picciotto in his climb to the hole, they kept at it. Later that afternoon, hours after they had been buried by the collapse of the north tower, Picciotto and those who had followed him stumbled onto the sidewalk and out of the rubble. Later that afternoon, fresh rescue workers would arrive on the scene. They helped Harris to safety, while those who had waited with her completed their own descent from the ruins of the twin towers. Like thousands of others, though perhaps more dramatically, this group had escaped death in the destruction of the World Trade Center.

Appendix

Documents Pertaining to Man-Made Disasters

Flight from the Cocoanut Grove Fire

One of the most catastrophic fires in American history took place in 1942, when a sudden blaze raced through the Cocoanut Grove nightclub in Boston. Nearly five hundred people were killed that night. Despite the intensity and the speed of the flames, though, many others managed to escape. This article, appearing in a Boston newspaper sixty years after the disaster, describes how some of the survivors fled to safety.

With flames surging behind them, panicked patrons rushed to the exit door at the top of the stairs, but it was locked to prevent folks from running out on their bills. They rushed to the revolving door at the main entrance, which soon jammed.

The Melody Lounge was consumed before people in the main dining room were even aware of trouble. When [patron Martin] Sheridan first heard the commotion, it sounded like shouts of "Fight, fight." Then he heard crackling flames and saw smoke.

"Let's get out of here," he snapped. "How about my mink coat?" his wife cried. "To hell with it," he answered.

They didn't get far. The lights went out and "it was like somebody conked you on the noggin," he recalled. Choking on fumes and smoke, the Sheridans passed out and sank to the floor in a pile of bodies.

The fire surged from the dining room into the new lounge. Many patrons there were trapped behind a vestibule door, which opened inward and had been slammed shut by the panicked crowd. Meanwhile, the staff managed to open a door in the dining room leading to Shawmut Street. Many escaped here, some with lungs so seared by the heat that they dropped dead in the street of pulmonary edema.

Others survived by jumping out of windows or hiding in the club's walk-in refrigerator. One Melody Lounge bartender survived by dropping to the floor and breathing through a wet towel as flames roared overhead.

Sheridan regained consciousness briefly on the club's floor. "I could hear people moaning, the sound of breaking glass, the sound of water running," he recalled. "I was shaking. I lay there, waiting for something. Then someone half-dragged and half-walked me out."

Stephanie Schorow, "Tragedy Haunts Hub 60 Years Later." *Boston Herald*, November 27, 2002.

Escape from a Train Wreck

Passenger trains do not crash often, but when they do the disasters are usually the subject of extensive media coverage. This excerpt, taken from a British newspaper article, tells of a 2001 crash in northern England, and describes how one of the passengers made her escape from the damaged passenger cars.

Miss [Janine] Edwards, an office worker, last night described the moments before and after the crash.

'I heard a noise of gravel under the wheels and thought at first it was snow on the rails but it was too loud for that.

'We had derailed and as the lights went out we went down the embankment. It was pitch black with things being thrown everywhere.

'All I could hear were screams as I held on to my table for dear life.

'When we stopped moving I looked round at the eight or ten people in our carriage.

'Three were injured, including a lady with a broken leg.' In front of her a man had been badly hurt as the window next to him shattered.

'Blood was pouring from his forehead while his wife held on to him and tried to staunch the flow with a towel.

'She stayed really calm.

'He looked as if he was bleeding to death. After the grinding noise of the rails and all the banging and crashing there was a sudden silence from the train, just people screaming for help and asking if everyone was OK.' Miss Edwards said she and her fellow passengers were trapped in coach D as both ends of it were crushed. In fact, the carriage had been hurled 40ft into a field. . . .

The coach had tipped on its side and there was a strong choking smell of diesel [fuel].

'I eventually got out through a window and down a ladder and was taken to a Portakabin [a temporary building] where it was warm.

'When I turned back and looked at the carriages all I could think of was how many people were in that train and how many were injured.'

"It's Me, Dad. The Train Just Crashed."
The Daily Mail (London), March 1, 2001.

Out from Under a Jeep

Not all accidents and disasters affect hundreds or thousands of people. This excerpt describes the escape of a young man from the wreckage of his overturned off-road vehicle. Like many other survivors who have escaped from tragedy over the years, this man was able to think calmly, quickly, and creatively, even under the most difficult of circumstances.

18-year-old former wrestler [Clancy Wright] was driving alone Oct. 2 [2003] at a popular off-road riding area about a quarter-mile from the southwestern Utah town in Beaver County when his open-air CJ-7 [Jeep] rolled, pinning his leg under a corner of the windshield and part of a roll bar. . . .

Wright was wearing a lap seat belt when the vehicle rolled and he was able to reach a jack in the vehicle. He said he tried three times to find the right placement for the jack on the ground and under the roll bar. He eventually was able to lift the Jeep enough to free himself.

"As the pressure released, I could feel the blood rush out of the leg," said Wright.

He said he never lost consciousness, even when he looked at his injured leg. All the skin, muscle and tissue in his left calf, from the knee to the ankle, was torn from the tibia and fibula bones. Both bones were completely exposed, but neither was fractured.

Wright said he wrapped everything back around the bones with his T-shirt.

Shortly afterward, he was found by Shay Goff of Minersville [Utah], who was riding ATVs [all-terrain vehicles] with family members in the area. Goff gave him a jacket to make a tourniquet, in an effort to stop the bleeding.

Mark Havnes, "Driver Pinned by Jeep Frees Self."
The Salt Lake Tribune, October 9, 2003.

Notes

Introduction:
Man-Made Disasters

1. Quoted in John Cloud, "A Miracle's Cost," *Time*, September 9, 2002, p. 39.

Chapter 1:
Escape from the *Titanic*

2. Quoted in Michael Davie, *Titanic: The Death and Life of a Legend*. New York: Alfred A. Knopf, 1987, p. 14.
3. Quoted in Daniel Allen Butler, *"Unsinkable": The Full Story*. Mechanicsburg, PA: Stackpole Books, 1998, p. 18.
4. Quoted in Walter Lord, *The Night Lives On*. New York: William Morrow, 1986, p. 29.
5. Quoted in Susan Wels, *Titanic: Legacy of the World's Greatest Ocean Liner*. San Diego: Tehabi Books, 1997, p. 49.
6. Violet Jessop, *Titanic Survivor*. Dobbs Ferry, NY: Sheridan House, 1997, p. 124.
7. Quoted in Lord, *The Night Lives On*, p. 241.

8. Quoted in Davie, *Titanic: The Death and Life of a Legend*, p. 55.
9. Quoted in Don Lynch and Ken Marschall, *Titanic: An Illustrated History*. New York: Hyperion, 1992, p. 100.
10. Jessop, *Titanic Survivor*, p. 127.
11. Quoted in Butler, *"Unsinkable*," p. 92.
12. Quoted in Wels, *Titanic: Legacy of the World's Greatest Ocean Liner*, p. 96.
13. Quoted in Butler, *"Unsinkable*," p. 118.
14. Quoted in Lynch and Marschall, *Titanic: An Illustrated History*, p. 129.
15. Jessop, *Titanic Survivor*, p. 132.
16. Quoted in Wels, *Titanic: Legacy of the World's Greatest Ocean Liner*, p. 103.
17. Quoted in Butler, *"Unsinkable*," p. 140.
18. Quoted in Butler, *"Unsinkable*," p. 133.
19. Quoted in Lynch and Marschall, *Titanic: An Illustrated History*, p. 148.

20. Jessop, *Titanic Survivor*, p. 139.

Chapter 2: Escape from Bhopal

21. Quoted in Matt Clark and Mariana Gosnell, "An Unstoppered Killer," *Newsweek,* December 17, 1984, p. 32.
22. Quoted in Sreekhant Khandekar and Suman Dubey, "Bhopal: City of Death," *India Today*, December 31, 1984, p. 6.
23. Quoted in Mark Whitaker et al., "'It Was Like Breathing Fire . . . ,'" *Newsweek*, December 17, 1984, p. 31.
24. Dan Kurzman, *A Killing Wind*. New York: McGraw-Hill, 1987, p. 25.
25. Quoted in Dominique Lapierre and Javier Moro, *Five Past Midnight in Bhopal*, trans. Kathryn Spink. New York: Warner Books, 2002, p. 187.
26. Quoted in Lapierre and Moro, *Five Past Midnight in Bhopal*, p. 286.
27. Quoted in Khandekar and Dubey, "Bhopal: City of Death," p. 9.
28. Quoted in Lapierre and Moro, *Five Past Midnight in Bhopal*, p. 297.
29. Quoted in Whitaker, "'It Was Like Breathing Fire . . . ,'" p. 27.
30. Quoted in Pico Iyer, "India's Night of Death," *Time*, December 17, 1984, p. 22.
31. Quoted in Khandekar and Dubey, "Bhopal: City of Death," p. 4.
32. Kurzman, *A Killing Wind*, p. 61.
33. Quoted in Lapierre and Moro, *Five Past Midnight in Bhopal*, p. 338.
34. Quoted in Khandekar and Dubey, "Bhopal: City of Death," p. 12.
35. Quoted in Khandekar and Dubey, "Bhopal: City of Death," p. 12.

Chapter 3: Escape from the *Hindenburg*

36. Quoted in Rick Archbold and Ken Marschall, *Hindenburg: An Illustrated History*. New York: Warner Communications, 1994, p. 162.
37. Harold G. Dick with Douglas H. Robinson, *The Golden Age of the Great Passenger Airships*, Washington, DC: Smithsonian Institution Press, 1985, p. 95.
38. Quoted in Archbold and Marschall, *Hindenburg*, p. 152.
39. Dick and Robinson, *The Golden Age of the Great Passenger Airships*, p. 138.
40. Quoted in Archbold and Marschall, *Hindenburg*, p. 178.
41. Quoted in Michael M. Mooney, *The Hindenburg*. New York: Dodd, Mead, 1972, p. 239.
42. Quoted in Archbold and Marschall, *Hindenburg*, p. 183
43. Quoted in Archbold and Marschall, *Hindenburg*, p. 183.
44. Quoted in Mooney, *The Hindenburg*, p. 243.
45. Quoted in Archbold and Marschall, *Hindenburg*, p. 187.
46. Quoted in Archbold and Marschall, *Hindenburg*, p. 188.
47. Margaret Mather, "I Was on the *Hindenburg*," *Harpers Monthly*, November 1933, p. 593.
48. Quoted in Mooney, *The Hindenburg*, p. 248.

Chapter 4: Three Mile Island

49. Quoted in Mark Stephens, *Three Mile Island.* New York: Random House, 1980, p. 73.

50. Quoted in PBS.org, "Meltdown at Three Mile Island," www.pbs.org.

51. Mike Gray and Ira Rosen, *The Warning.* New York: W.W. Norton, 1982, p. 231.

52. Quoted in Robert Del Tredici, *The People of Three Mile Island.* San Francisco: Sierra Club Books, 1980, p. 31.

53. Quoted in Gray and Rosen, *The Warning*, p. 221.

54. Quoted in Del Tredici, *The People of Three Mile Island*, p. 45.

55. Quoted in Stephens, *Three Mile Island*, p. 149.

56. Quoted in Del Tredici, *The People of Three Mile Island*, p. 39.

57. Quoted in Del Tredici, *The People of Three Mile Island*, p. 39.

58. Quoted in Stephens, *Three Mile Island*, p. 188.

59. Quoted in Del Tredici, *The People of Three Mile Island*, p. 39.

60. Quoted in PBS.org, "Meltdown at Three Mile Island," p. 13.

61. Quoted in Daniel F. Ford, *Three Mile Island: Thirty Minutes to Meltdown.* New York: Penguin Books, 1981, p. 221.

62. Quoted in Stephens, *Three Mile Island*, p. 163.

63. Quoted in Del Tredici, *The People of Three Mile Island*, p. 39.

64. Quoted in Gray and Rosen, *The Warning*, p. 211.

65. Quoted in Del Tredici, *The People of Three Mile Island*, p. 43.

66. Quoted in Del Tredici, *The People of Three Mile Island*, p. 102.

67. Wilborn Hampton, *Meltdown.* Cambridge, MA: Candlewick Press, 2001, p. 42.

68. Quoted in Hampton, *Meltdown*, p. 74.

Chapter 5: Escape from the World Trade Center

69. Quoted in Richard Bernstein, *Out of the Blue.* New York: Times Books, 2002, p. 199.

70. Quoted in Allison Gilbert et al., eds., *Covering Catastrophe: Broadcast Journalists Report September 11.* Chicago: Bonus Books, 2002, p. 8.

71. Richard Picciotto, *Last Man Down.* New York: Berkley Books, 2002, p. 15.

72. Quoted in Bernstein, *Out of the Blue*, p. 202.

73. Quoted in Salon.com, *Afterwords.* New York: Washington Square Press, 2002, p. 3.

74. Quoted in Mitchell Fink and Lois Mathias, *Never Forget.* New York: Regan Books, 2002, p. 54.

75. Quoted in Bernstein, *Out of the Blue*, p. 201.

76. Quoted in Fink and Mathias, *Never Forget*, p. 47.

77. Quoted in Fink and Mathias, *Never Forget*, p. 126.

78. Quoted in Fink and Mathias, *Never Forget*, p. 117.

79. Quoted in Fink and Mathias, *Never Forget*, p. 49.

80. Quoted in Dennis Smith, *Report from Ground Zero*. New York: Viking, 2002, p. 72.

81. Quoted in Gilbert, *Covering Catastrophe*, p. 75.

82. Quoted in Tom Barbash, *On Top of the World*. New York: HarperCollins, 2003, pp. 16–17.

83. Quoted in Cloud, "A Miracle's Cost," p. 37.

84. Picciotto, *Last Man Down*, p. 109.

85. Quoted in Smith, *Report from Ground Zero*, p. 79.

For Further Reading

Books

Robert D. Ballard, *Exploring the Titanic.* New York: Scholastic, 1988. An illustrated history of the *Titanic*, including information on the disaster and the later discovery of the wrecked ship on the ocean floor.

Michael D. Cole, *Three Mile Island: Nuclear Disaster.* Berkeley Heights, NJ: Enslow, 2002. A description of the 1979 Three Mile Island catastrophe.

Lee Davis, *Man-Made Catastrophes: From the Burning of Rome to the Lockerbie Crash.* New York: Facts On File, 1993. About man-made disasters throughout history.

Arthur Diamond, *The Bhopal Chemical Leak.* San Diego: Lucent Books, 1990. An informative book about the disaster in Bhopal, written not long after the gas leak took place.

Howell Raines, ed., *A Nation Challenged: A Visual History of 9/11 and Its Aftermath.* New York: Scholastic, 2002.

A pictorial description, with text, of the September 11, 2001, disaster. Particular emphasis on the World Trade Center.

Shelley Tanaka, *The Disaster of the Hindenburg: The Last Flight of the Greatest Airship Ever Built.* New York: Scholastic/Madison Press Books, 1993. About the crash of the *Hindenburg*, including discussion of the possible causes of the disaster.

Websites

Navy Lakehurst Historical Society (www.nlhs.com). Information about the *Hindenburg* and its last flight.

September 11, 2001 News Archives (www.september11news.com). News archives of material related to the September 11, 2001, attacks on the World Trade Center and elsewhere. Many useful links as well.

Titanic Historical Society (www.titanic 1.org). Includes information about the ship and passengers, along with links to other useful related sites.

Works Consulted

Books

Rick Archbold and Ken Marschall, *Hindenburg: An Illustrated History.* New York: Warner Communications, 1994. A beautifully illustrated coffee-table book about the *Hindenburg.* Well written and informative.

Tom Barbash, *On Top of the World.* New York: HarperCollins, 2003. The deaths—and occasional escape—of workers at one company headquartered in the World Trade Center.

Richard Bernstein, *Out of the Blue.* New York: Times Books, 2002. A valuable and thorough description of the events of September 11, 2001.

Daniel Allen Butler, *"Unsinkable": The Full Story.* Mechanicsburg, PA: Stackpole Books, 1998. A good source for information on the *Titanic* and its sinking.

Michael Davie, *Titanic: The Death and Life of a Legend.* New York: Alfred A. Knopf, 1987. A thorough history of the *Titanic.* Informative.

Robert Del Tredici, *The People of Three Mile Island.* San Francisco: Sierra Club Books, 1980. A fascinating book of interviews with people who lived near Three Mile Island, along with valuable background information on the plant and its history. Very informative and often quite moving.

Harold G. Dick with Douglas H. Robinson, *The Golden Age of the Great Passenger Airships.* Washington, DC: Smithsonian Institution Press, 1985. The author was involved with the building and testing of two famous German airships, one of them the *Hindenburg.*

Mitchell Fink and Lois Mathias, *Never Forget.* New York: Regan Books, 2002. Interviews with survivors, observers, and rescue personnel affected by the terrorist attacks of September 11, 2001. Interesting and emotional.

Daniel F. Ford, *Three Mile Island: Thirty Minutes to Meltdown.* New York: Penguin Books, 1981. A description of the nuclear accident at Three Mile

Island and how it was handled. Focuses mainly on the disaster and the discussions among political leaders, scientists, and emergency personnel.

Allison Gilbert et al., eds., *Covering Catastrophe: Broadcast Journalists Report September 11.* Chicago: Bonus Books, 2002. Memories and experiences of broadcast journalists who covered the events of September 11, 2001.

Mike Gray and Ira Rosen, *The Warning.* New York: W.W. Norton, 1982. An investigation of the nuclear accident at Three Mile Island.

Wilborn Hampton, *Meltdown.* Cambridge, MA: Candlewick Press, 2001. A reporter's account of his experiences covering the Three Mile Island disaster.

Violet Jessop, *Titanic Survivor.* Dobbs Ferry, NY: Sheridan House, 1997. Jessop was a stewardess aboard the *Titanic.* This is her edited memoir, which includes a few pages describing the accident and her experiences escaping from the sinking ship.

Dan Kurzman, *A Killing Wind.* New York: McGraw-Hill, 1987. A well-written, well-researched account of the Bhopal tragedy and its aftermath. Based on extensive research and interviews with survivors.

Dominique Lapierre and Javier Moro, *Five Past Midnight in Bhopal.* Trans. Kathryn Spink. New York: Warner Books, 2002. Some useful information about the Bhopal tragedy, although much does not directly relate to the tragedy itself, and there are many fictionalized conversations.

Walter Lord, *The Night Lives On.* New York: William Morrow, 1986. Thoughts about the *Titanic* from one of the world's leading authorities.

———, *A Night to Remember.* New York: Holt, Rinehart and Winston, 1955. A relatively short and very readable account of the *Titanic* and the disaster it experienced. This book rekindled enthusiasm for the subject when it first was published.

Don Lynch and Ken Marschall, *Titanic: An Illustrated History.* New York: Hyperion, 1992. A beautifully illustrated book with valuable information about the *Titanic.*

Michael M. Mooney, *The Hindenburg.* New York: Dodd, Mead, 1972. A thorough account of the *Hindenburg* and its last flight. Includes many fictionalized conversations.

Richard Picciotto, *Last Man Down.* New York: Berkley Books, 2002. Picciotto was a firefighter who made a particularly dramatic escape from the wreckage of the twin towers. This is his own account of what happened.

Salon.com, *Afterwords.* New York: Washington Square Press, 2002. A book of readings on various aspects of the September 11, 2001, terrorist attacks.

Dennis Smith, *Report from Ground Zero.* New York: Viking, 2002. About the rescue efforts at the World Trade Center. Interviews with commentary, and includes personal reflections. Well written and informative.

Mark Stephens, *Three Mile Island.* New York: Random House, 1980. Stephens was a member of a commission that investigated what happened in the disaster at Three Mile Island. His account is thorough and includes useful information about those who escaped—and why.

Susan Wels, *Titanic: Legacy of the World's Greatest Ocean Liner.* San Diego: Tehabi Books, 1997. A nicely illustrated book with useful information about the *Titanic.*

World Almanac and Book of Facts 2003. New York: World Almanac Books, 2003. Useful facts and figures.

Periodicals
Matt Clark and Mariana Gosnell, "An Unstoppered Killer," *Newsweek,* December 17, 1984.

John Cloud, "A Miracle's Cost," *Time,* September 9, 2002.

Pico Iyer, "India's Night of Death," *Time,* December 17, 1984.

Sreekhant Khandekar and Suman Dubey, "Bhopal: City of Death," *India Today,* December 31, 1984.

John S. Lang, "India's Tragedy—A Warning Heard Around the World," *U.S. News & World Report,* December 17, 1984.

Margaret Mather, "I Was on the *Hindenburg,*" *Harpers Monthly,* November 1933.

PBS.org, "Meltdown at Three Mile Island." www.pbs.org.

Mark Whitaker et al., "'It Was Like Breathing Fire . . . ,'" *Newsweek,* December 17, 1984.

Index

Picture Credits

About the Author

Stephen Currie is the creator of Lucent's Great Escapes series. He has also written many other books for children and young adults, among them *Life in the Trenches* and *Terrorists and Terrorist Groups*, both for Lucent. He lives in New York State with his wife and children. Among his hobbies are kayaking, snowshoeing, and bicycling.